Having Something to Say When You Have to Say Something

Having Something to Say When You Have to Say Something

The Art of Organizing Your Presentation

Randy Horn

SkillPath Publications
Mission, KS

Editor: Kelly Scanlon

Page Layout: Premila Malik Borchardt and Rod Hankins

Cover Design: Rod Hankins

ISBN: 1-57294-066-2

Library of Congress Catalog Card Number: 96-68755

10 9 8 7 6 5 4 3   05   06   07

Printed in the United States of America

For Ashley,

Who loved having an audience

Contents

Contents

Acknowledgments

I've had many excellent coaches in the art of public speaking and presenting. They began with youth group leaders in church and Boy Scouts, continued with speech teachers in high school, college, and graduate school, and most recently have been the good and able people at SkillPath. But my deepest appreciation is reserved for my audiences who over the years let me learn the art of presentation by presenting to them. Their support, encouragement, and patience helped me grow through my mistakes. I am also deeply grateful to my wife, Laura, and my children, Travis, Josh, and Eva, for their patient support in spite of having to endure my speeches around the house for years.

Chapter One

The Pain, Process, and Payoffs of Preparation

So, you've been asked to say something. Perhaps it's nothing more than a few brief remarks at an upcoming luncheon. Maybe it's a technical presentation to a project team. Maybe it's a public relations talk at a community organization. Or maybe it's the keynote address at the annual meeting of your professional society.

But whether it involves a big or small audience, whether it is relatively inconsequential or one of those career makers/breakers, you wouldn't be reading this book if you didn't want to do a good job. Where do you start in improving your presentations? Begin by taking the quiz on the next page.

Self-Assessment

Answer True or False to the following questions:

1. _____ I often feel at a loss about how to start getting a presentation together.

2. _____ I usually procrastinate when it comes to preparing for presentations.

3. _____ I feel I know the information, but I have a hard time focusing on what I want to say.

4. _____ I am concerned about keeping my presentation interesting and not losing people's attention.

5. _____ I think my presentations are okay, but feel they lack polish and precision.

6. _____ I find it difficult to wind things down and wrap them up.

7. _____ I hate researching and organizing information.

8. _____ I'd rather walk on hot coals than give a presentation!

If you answered "True" to two or more of the above statements, then this book is definitely for you!

As a presenter, you have the opportunity to communicate information, change minds, influence people's thinking, motivate, and inspire. You also have the opportunity to fail. What will make the difference? How can you assure yourself that you'll do a good job, that you'll communicate well, and that you'll do so with confidence? In other words, how can you be sure you'll have something to say when it comes time to say something?

The threefold secret to successful presentations is this: preparation, preparation, preparation! More and more business and professional people are being called upon to present—to clients and customers, project teams, management, the general public, stockholders, special interest groups, and community groups. Knowing how to present well is a basic survival skill for those who want to move ahead in their organization and in their career. And the single most important ingredient to successful presentations is preparation.

A noted public speaker was contacted about making a presentation, but the caller was concerned because his organization was seeking someone at the last minute.

"How long will it take you to prepare?" the anxious event coordinator asked.

"That depends," the speaker replied. "If you want me to talk for an hour or two, I can come right now. If you want me to talk for thirty minutes, then I'll need at least a day to prepare. And if you want me to talk for ten minutes or less, then I'll need a week to prepare!"

Precision, crispness, clarity, interest—all of these qualities require preparation, whether you're talking for ten minutes or two hours. Almost anyone can get up and ramble. You've probably had the unfortunate experience of sitting through an unfocused, unorganized presentation that seemed to go on interminably. Perhaps you've also had the good fortune of hearing an interesting, entertaining, concise, and lively presentation recently.

In our MTV culture, long speeches are the exception. Most people's attention spans have been culturally conditioned to be quite short, so the days of lengthy orations are, for the most part, a thing of history. But the key difference between success and failure in business presentations is not the amount of time the speaker talks. Ten minutes is nine minutes too long for some speakers, while others can carry an audience an entire day. The key difference between failure and success when it comes to presentations is as simple and as challenging as this: thorough preparation.

The Pain of Preparation

The meeting is tomorrow. The dreaded day has drawn nigh. Jan sits at her desk at home, staring at the computer screen. "How could I have put this off so long?" she asks herself. "Good grief, I've known I was going to have to talk to the account management team for over a month. But here I am, as usual, at the last minute, trying to pull my thoughts together."

She stares at the screen, but no words magically appear. Worse, no words shape themselves into intelligible sentences in her head. Her mind seems as blank as the screen. An array of charts and figures are scattered about. The minutes tick by. The task can be postponed no longer. Jan must prepare her presentation tonight—right now. "Next time," she murmurs to herself, "next time, I'll get started earlier."

Given the absolute necessity of preparation to a successful presentation, why do so many people fail to prepare? Why did Jan put off her preparation? In one word: Pain.

There's nothing easy about preparing for a presentation. It requires thought, reflection, discipline, diligence, and hard work. None of these comes easily, not even to a seasoned presenter. Furthermore, most people have received little or no training in how to prepare a presentation. Maybe you took a public speaking class in high school or college. But that may seem like a long time ago—and what you learned may be long-forgotten. The bad news is, it takes work to prepare.

Use Exercise #1 to identify your preparation "pain points."

If the bad news is that preparation can be a pain, the good news is this: It is a skill you can learn. It is also a skill well worth learning. As you learn the process of organizing your presentations, you'll find that the pain of preparation yields large payoffs—personally and professionally. Not everyone is destined to be a world renowned orator, but everyone can master the basics of preparing a good presentation. You *can* learn how to put together a clear, concise, interesting, and informative presentation. That's what this book is all about.

Exercise #1:

Identify Your Pain Points

Knowing your enemy is half the battle. Which of the following make preparation difficult for you? Put a check mark by those that apply to you. Then go back and circle your number one pain point.

☐ Don't know where to begin ☐ Can't narrow topic down

☐ Finding the time to prepare ☐ Lack of confidence

☐ Disorganization ☐ Notice too short

☐ Focusing on the key idea ☐ Don't know how to illustrate

☐ Can't figure out how to open ☐ Lack of information

☐ Unsure about how to close ☐ Fear of audience response

☐ Don't want to do it ☐ Drawing a blank

☐ Other: _____

The Process of Preparation

The pain of preparation is much diminished when you have a predictable, proven process to follow. One of the greatest difficulties many people face in preparing a presentation is not knowing how or where to start. That is at the root of much of the procrastination that plagues presenters. But having a logical, clear process to follow helps overcome that obstacle. As you learn and practice the process of preparation this book teaches, you will find it becomes easier and easier and the pain and hard work less and less.

The reality is, of course, that there is no one right way to prepare a presentation. Some people begin with their conclusion and work backwards. Others focus first on their opening and on how to establish initial contact with the audience. Still others develop the main body of their presentation first and then work on the opening and closing. But having said this, the fact remains that there is an approach to preparation that generally seems to work best for most people. All good presenters have this in common: they have a *systematic* method of preparation that guides them through the process.

Step by step, this book will lead you through a proven process of preparation. You'll learn how to get started and how to narrow your focus. You'll get tips on gathering and organizing your material and ways to make it interesting and memorable. You'll also look at openings, endings, transitions, and ways to prepare for the unpredictable. Finally, you'll look at how to put it all together and to begin to reap the payoffs of your preparation. Two tools will help you with this process: exercises and Apply It Now! practices. The exercises help reinforce your understanding of specific concepts presented in the book. Apply It Now! practices give you an opportunity to prepare an actual presentation as you work through this book.

The Payoffs of Preparation

Thorough preparation is essential for quality presentations. It also yields many payoffs—both personally and professionally. Exercise 2 will guide you in identifying the payoffs you reap from taking the time to prepare your presentation.

Keep the payoffs that are important to you in mind as you work your way through this book. Refer back to Exercise 2 when you're tempted to skimp on the preparation or think it might be easier just to "wing it." Remember, preparation is the behind-the-scenes work that sets the stage for the success of your presentation.

Exercise #2:

Identify Your Preparation Payoffs

Which of the following payoffs are important to you? Put a 1, 2, and 3 next to the three payoffs that are most important to you *personally*. Circle the three that are most important to you *professionally*.

___ Less stress and worry	___ Feeling of being in control
___ Self-confidence	___ Increased productivity
___ Respect of peers	___ More opportunities to present
___ Recognition of supervisor	___ Opportunities to advance
___ Opportunity to be creative	___ Minimizes last-minute panic
___ Allows time to refine, polish	___ Can better organize presentation
___ Know what you're talking about	___ Other_____

Begin now to build a mental picture of yourself as a successful presenter. See yourself stepping before the audience with confidence and self-assurance. Picture yourself delivering a clear, concise, informative, and entertaining presentation. Feel the energy flowing between you and your listeners. Their eyes are on you. They are with you, listening and absorbing what you have to say. You hear the confidence in your voice and you feel your anxiousness being channeled into energy for the audience. You illustrate a key point with a humorous story. Listen to their laughter as they respond to you. You finish your presentation. There is a round of applause as you take your seat, basking in the glow of a job well done.

Visualizing your success isn't magic. But it does help you to begin seeing yourself as a successful presenter. Mentally embrace the payoff as you enter into the process of preparation and all the accompanying hard work.

"The key difference between failure and success in presentations is as simple and as challenging as this: thorough preparation."

Apply It Now!

Identify the Pain, Process, and Payoffs of Preparation

Think about a presentation you will soon face. Use this upcoming talk as your own personal case study throughout this book. Write out your answers to the following questions now.

1. Name your *pain* factor. What is difficult for you in preparing this presentation?

   _____

   _____

   _____

2. Where are you in the *process?* How have you already started preparation?

   _____

   _____

   _____

3. What *payoffs* might this presentation yield for you?

   _____

   _____

   _____

Key Idea Chart

1. The key to successful presentations can be summed up in one word: Preparation.

2. Successful preparation involves the three "P's": Pain, Process, and Payoff.

3. There is more than one correct way to approach the process of preparation, but having a systematic approach to preparation is helpful.

4. Visualizing your success as a presenter can be useful in preparing.

5. Write out below the key idea you got for yourself from this chapter.

_____

_____

_____

_____

_____

_____

_____

_____

_____

Chapter Two

Tools for Getting Started

Two months ago, James was assigned the responsibility of presenting a plan to the department heads. The plan was to recommend a reallocation of support staff. He's done his homework. He understands why a change is necessary, and he believes he's come up with some good ideas. He has a mountain of data and information, along with some specific recommendations he wants to make. As the date of his presentation gets closer, however, the question that haunts James is this: "How can I organize all this information? Where do I begin?"

Where do you start when you have to get ready to make a presentation? What are the steps involved in organizing a clear, concise, powerful talk? Is it best to begin at the beginning, the middle, the end, or somewhere in between? Do you start with an outline, an illustration, a goal statement, or do you simply get going by gathering material?

As mentioned in Chapter 1, there's no one right way to prepare, but most successful presenters follow some sort of systematic plan to help them get ready.

Preparing a presentation is a lot like hugging an elephant. There's a lot to get a hold of and it's not clear where it's best to grab on!

Consider this: When faced with hugging the Preparation Elephant, where do you usually grab hold? Which of the following most closely describes your style? Do you usually first grab hold of:

- The tail? Do you think in terms of the end goal, the results you're after?

- The trunk? Do you think in terms of the front end—getting started, getting people's attention?

- The tusks? Do you like to identify the pointed issues that must be dealt with?

- A leg? Do you focus on the supportive, substantial material?

- The ears? Do you focus on the audience and their questions?

Having a plan of preparation in mind helps you overcome one of the biggest obstacles to successful preparation—the propensity to put it off. Approaching the problem of preparation in an organized fashion can help you overcome procrastination and get you moving toward success.

This book will take you through a process of preparation that is detailed and specific. But before you get into those details, it's best to think about the big picture.

Have you ever worked a jigsaw puzzle? What's the first thing you do when you start putting the puzzle together? Most people turn the pieces over and then begin looking for the straight edges, the pieces that form the border. Especially important, of course, are the corner pieces. Next, some people plunge right in, beginning to fit together pieces of matching color. But the seasoned jigsaw puzzler knows that before you tackle the details, it's very important to look at the picture on the box! You need the big picture so you can organize the detail work.

There are three big-picture factors to consider as you prepare your presentation:

- Your audience—the "who"

- Your purpose—the "why"

- The occasion—the "where"

Knowing Your Audience—The Who

While the heart of your message might be the same, there is a world of difference between presenting to twelve and to twelve hundred. Likewise, presenting before a sympathetic audience is different than presenting before a questioning or belligerent audience.

Pity poor Pete! He thought he would be sharing the technical paper he'd presented at a professional conference to a handful of his fellow computer wizards. Imagine his surprise when he found more than two dozen managers and supervisors crowded into the conference room, eagerly awaiting a general summary of the key issues to come out of the recent conference he'd attended. Pete was well prepared. The problem was he was prepared for the wrong audience!

Taking time to think about your audience is a good place to begin the process of preparation. This step is as simple as asking, "To whom will I be presenting?" Having a mental image of the group you'll be talking to allows your subconscious to work on the material as you gather it, shaping it to the needs of your listeners. Consider the many factors there are to know about your audience:

- Size

- Educational background

- Sympathy or hostility quotient

- Gender make-up

- Racial or ethnic configuration

- Felt-needs and questions

- History with you as a presenter

- Socioeconomic status

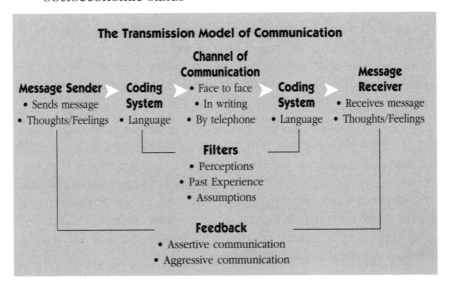

The Transmission Model of Communication

Message Sender	Coding System	Channel of Communication	Coding System	Message Receiver
• Sends message		• Face to face		• Receives message
• Thoughts/Feelings	• Language	• In writing	• Language	• Thoughts/Feelings
		• By telephone		

Filters
- Perceptions
- Past Experience
- Assumptions

Feedback
- Assertive communication
- Aggressive communication

Why is it so important to know your audience? In order to answer that question, you must understand the transmission model of communication. This model says that you begin with a message in your mind that you want to transmit to another person or a group. You encode that message in words, symbols, sounds, and body language. You then transmit your message to your audience via words, written communication, gestures, pictures, or other means. The audience, in turn, decodes it. Then they have a message in their minds. Good communication has occurred when the message the audience has "decoded" is the same as the one you intended.

The formula is I + P = C:

Intention + Perception = Communication

Whatever the sender's intention, the crucial element in this formula is what the listener perceives. Consider the following sign spotted in a dry cleaner's window:

> **Drop your pants here**
>
> **and you'll receive**
>
> **immediate attention!**

Clearly, the owner of the establishment intended one communication, but most people perceived another!

Thinking carefully about your audience helps minimize misperceptions. As you identify their needs, questions, expectations, and assumptions, you'll become more aware of the filters and static that may be on the line. And it helps you tailor the way you communicate to fit your particular audience.

After all, a good presenter doesn't count on the audience to do all the work of listening. In addition to fashioning an interesting and engaging presentation, the good presenter also anticipates the audience's needs and concerns and tailors the presentation to address them.

Think of yourself as an audience member. Which of the following questions do you ask yourself while listening to a presenter?

- Is what I'm hearing true?

- Is this relevant to my concerns?

- Does it make good sense?

- What's in this for me?

- So what? Who cares?

If you ask yourself some of these kinds of questions when you're in the audience, it's probably safe to assume that your listeners will be silently asking the same kinds of questions of you the next time you present.

If you know the individuals you will be presenting to, begin now to picture them. See their individual faces, not just the group. Visualize them really tuned in and listening to you. If you don't know your audience personally, then picture them as accurately as you can, based on the data you have about them. Are they young or old? Business associates or customers? A small intimate gathering or an auditorium full of people? See them as an interested group of people paying close attention to you and your presentation.

Keep this mental picture of your audience in the back of your thoughts as you prepare. Let it screen the material you gather and guide you as you organize your presentation.

There may be times, of course, when you will be presenting the same material to several different audiences. In that case, you'll need to either fashion your presentation in a way that will be suitable for a variety of audiences or fine-tune it to fit each audience.

The important thing to keep in mind at this point is that you will be presenting to particular people with particular biases, histories, assumptions, questions, needs, and interests. A roomful of working mothers presents a different challenge than an audience of retirees. Know your audience members and let them be the backdrop against which you prepare. This is an essential part of the big picture of preparation.

A detailed "Audience Awareness Checklist" is included in Appendix A, page 177. Refer to it as you begin the process of preparation.

"A journey of a thousand miles begins with a single step."
—Lao Tsu

Defining Your Purpose—The Why

Another important tool for getting started is thinking through these kinds of questions:

- What's the purpose?

- Why am I making this presentation?

- What do I hope to accomplish?

Do you want to inform, entertain, convince, persuade, inspire, motivate, sell, or achieve some combination of these?

Chapter 3 will look more closely at the issue of defining your purpose. A written purpose statement, in fact, is an essential step in solid preparation. But for now, think in broad categories. Why are you making this presentation? What is the goal or end you aim toward? Many business presentations center on one of two purposes—to inform or to persuade.

Informing

The primary purpose of your presentation may be to communicate information. You know some things that others need to know. Often, an oral presentation is deemed the most effective way to share that information. The lecture remains the mainstay of most schools, and it has its place in business forums as well.

Sue does many presentations in her work as public relations coordinator. She frequently appears before audiences in her own company as well as in the larger community. Internally, she seeks to build morale and to encourage employees to take part in public service activities. Externally, she strives to build goodwill for the company and never misses an opportunity to underscore the significant contributions the company makes to the community. She is, of course, being persuasive. But her main focus is education. She is intent on providing accurate, timely, and clear information that will maximize goodwill for the business.

Persuading

Equally frequent in business settings are presentations where the persuasive element is foremost. Whether it is persuading a client to renew a contract, convincing a customer to purchase new merchandise, or selling management on a new proposal, the bottom line is convincing someone of something—usually something that requires action.

Dan is a bidder and contract writer for a commercial construction company. He often makes presentations to prospective clients, seeking their business and trying to persuade them to give his company a shot at the work. In these presentations, Dan delivers a great deal of clear, factual data—information, yes—but the bottom line is, Dan is selling. He wants to persuade his clients to act.

As you begin preparing your presentations, you must begin to clarify your main purpose in your own mind. Doing so will not only shape the content of your presentation, it will also shape the way you organize and develop your material.

Exercise #3:

Finding the Main Purpose

Surf through the television channels tonight. Pause at the news, a documentary, a situation comedy, a religious program, public television, a home shopping channel, or a political discussion. Label the main purpose of each program. Is the show you're watching primarily seeking to entertain, inform, inspire, or sell? What differences in style and format distinguish the presentations according to their respective purposes?

Type of Program	Purpose	Style/Format
_____	_____	_____
_____	_____	_____
_____	_____	_____
_____	_____	_____
_____	_____	_____
_____	_____	_____
_____	_____	_____

Fitting the Occasion—The Where

The "where" question isn't concerned so much about geographic location and physical setting (although having an idea of the actual physical environment in which your presentation will be made is important) as it is with identifying the kind of occasion at which you'll be presenting. Will it be a sales meeting? board meeting? fund-raising campaign? Considering the occasion of your presentation is, of course, closely related to identifying your audience and purpose, but with a slightly different focus. In thinking about your audience, you are considering factors such as size, age, background, interests, and so forth. When you are thinking in terms of the purpose of your presentation, you are focusing on your goal— what you want to accomplish. But when you think about the occasion of your presentation, you are thinking about the social context in which you will present.

A detailed, technical presentation fits the occasion of a project team meeting, but it would be woefully out of place at an after-hours get together. Inspired oratory might well fill the bill at a planning retreat with senior managers or at an annual recognition banquet, but it probably would be out of place in a weekly staff meeting.

As you begin the process of preparation, you will want to think not only strategically (your purpose) and empathetically (your audience's needs) but also socially (the occasion). The nature of the occasion shapes the content of your presentation as well as the tone or tenor of it. Some occasions demand sobriety and formality. Others lend themselves to levity and a casual style.

Exercise #4:

Occasions for Presentations

Look over the list below and put a check mark next to those situations in which you have made presentations. Then go back and put an "X" by the situations that you would find most challenging and difficult.

☐ Business briefing (small group)

☐ Classroom lecture

☐ Sales presentation to client(s)

☐ Eulogy of a friend

☐ Motivational talk

☐ New employee training

☐ Roast of a friend or associate

☐ Technical presentation

☐ Fund-raising presentation

☐ Other _____

☐ Keynote address (large group)

☐ Training/seminar

☐ Proposal to management team

☐ Civic club or organization

☐ Budget presentation to board

☐ Computer training class

☐ Honorary or retiree banquet

☐ Church or support group

☐ Formal oration/Toastmasters

Take a risk. Pick one of those occasions you put an "X" next to and seek an opportunity to stretch yourself by making a presentation in that forum.

Most of the skills involved in preparing a presentation for one occasion readily carry over to other occasions and situations, requiring only some fine-tuning and adjustment. But it is important as you begin your preparation that you have the specific occasion and its social setting in mind. This will help you zero in on the most suitable structure for your presentation, appropriate illustrations, and other factors such as your opening and conclusion.

The good news is this: If you can master the art of presenting to twelve people, you can learn to present confidently and competently to twelve hundred. The basic principles are the same. You get started in your preparation by thinking about your audience and its needs, your goal and purpose for the presentation, and the social setting or occasion of your talk. Let these three factors form the mental backdrop against which you construct your presentation. They will guide your research, your study, and most important of all—your creativity.

Back to poor Pete, who had walked into a situation far different than the one he had anticipated. Pete pulled it off and he pulled it off potently. He quickly realized he'd misunderstood not only who his audience would be, but also the purpose and the occasion of his presentation. But he had done his homework. In preparing for his technical presentation at the conference, he had researched the background factors the managers and supervisors were most concerned with. In addition, he'd approached the conference professionally, attending the general sessions and picking up a lot of information in informal settings. Pete was an experienced presenter. He was rattled to be sure. But he quietly put his technical report back in his folder and proceeded to extemporaneously offer a clear and concise report on the conference, supplemented with plenty of time for questions and answers. He was able to do so because he'd taken the time to thoroughly prepare.

You can too! You can learn to present clearly and powerfully, even when circumstances throw you a curve. How? Embrace the discipline of preparation not as a harsh taskmaster, but as a friend who will clear a path to smooth presentations. Begin now to train yourself to start thinking about the who, the why, and the where of your presentation as soon as the opportunity appears on the horizon.

Apply It Now!

The Who, the Why, and the Where

Think about the case study presentation you identified in Chapter 1.

1. Who will your audience be?

   _____

   Now, turn to the "Audience Awareness Checklist" in Appendix A, page 177, and complete that worksheet as it applies to your upcoming presentation.

2. Think about the "why" of your presentation. Will you be seeking primarily to inspire, persuade, inform, or entertain? Complete the following sentence: The main thing I will be doing in this presentation is:

   _____

3. Where will you be presenting? What is the occasion for this presentation? Will it be to a large or small group? In a formal or an informal setting? Write below a brief description of the occasion.

   _____

   _____

   _____

   _____

Key Idea Chart

1. Three background factors that must be considered in preparing for a presentation are:

   - Audience—the Who

   - Purpose—the Why

   - Occasion—the Where

2. There are many ways to prepare; the key is having a systematic plan.

3. The formula for good communication is $I + P = C$. This means that your Intention plus your listener's Perception equals the act of Communication.

4. Write out below the key idea you got for yourself from Chapter 2.

   _____

   _____

   _____

   _____

   _____

   _____

   _____

   _____

Narrowing Your Focus

How many times have you sat through a presentation asking yourself, "Where is this going? What's the point? What's this speaker getting at?" And how many times have you left a presentation still not knowing the answer to those questions? Or, you may have left mentally long before you got to leave physically.

In this chapter, you will look at two very powerful tools that will help you know where you're going with your presentation. The first tool focuses on your content. The second on your audience. Together, they will help you narrow your focus and provide a structure for your presentation.

The Importance of Getting Specific

In the last chapter, you looked at the importance of defining your purpose in a general sort of way. That is the starting point, of course—to be clear about your overall objective. Will you be informing, persuading, inspiring, training, or just what? Having identified your general purpose, you must get specific. What, exactly, do you hope to accomplish in the presentation?

If you want to inform, what do you want to inform about? For what reasons? To what end?

Is your intention to persuade? In what regard? to buy, to sell, or to negotiate? to think differently? to act differently? feel differently? Some combination of all of these?

Do you hope to inspire? Why? For what goal or purpose? To what end?

Disciplining yourself to ask and answer these kinds of questions can be hard work. But it's a very necessary step in having something to say. If you're not clear about the main point of your presentation, you can be sure your audience won't be either. *If it's fuzzy to you, it will be fuzzy to them.*

So how do you get rid of the fuzzies? How do you narrow your focus? How do you get specific about what you hope to accomplish? By asking yourself the right questions!

There is, first, the question about *content: What is your main point?*

Then, there is the question about the *impact* you want to have on your listeners: *How are you asking your audience to change?*

The first question centers on what you want to communicate to your audience. The second centers on what you want your audience to do with what you've communicated. Let's look at the content issue first.

Identifying Your Main Point

There sits Fred. It's only Monday morning, but Thursday afternoon looms ominously on the horizon. Thursday is when Fred has to introduce the new marketing plan to the rest of the department. There's a lot to cover. Ways the new plan improves on the old one. Changes it will require from the sales staff. New goals and guidelines. The necessity of adjusting some time lines and budget priorities. As he pores over the pages and charts and data, Fred feels awash in facts and figures. Where will he ever begin? How's he ever going to get a handle on organizing all this information?

Have you ever felt that way? Probably so. Most presenters do at times. It's easy to feel overwhelmed when you're facing the prospect of organizing a presentation—especially one that might entail a great deal of new information or data. But if you are to present with clarity and power, if you are going to have something to say, you are going to need to find a way to cut through all that information and get right to the heart of the matter.

The way to do that is to persistently ask yourself this question: "What is your main point?" And you keep on asking yourself that question in a variety of forms until you come up with a concise, clear, simple answer.

- What's the one, single, most important idea you want to get across?

- What's the key piece of information you'll be presenting?

- What's your thesis or main contention?

- What's the heart of your presentation?

- If you had to reduce your presentation to one sentence, what would it be?

The key to making these questions work is to write out your answer. Until you can write your main point in one simple, declarative sentence, you haven't really narrowed your focus sufficiently. There will be time later on to expand your subject, to add points, to fill in with details, color, and illustration. But now is the time to distill and concentrate. Discipline yourself to take the time to put your main point down on paper.

Fred makes his first stab at it. He writes on his legal pad: "My main point is that the new marketing plan has been thoroughly researched and tested, represents state-of-the-art thinking, ought to increase sales significantly, and while it will require some adjustments for all of us, it should be a great improvement."

Nice try, Fred, but you don't win the prize yet.

What's wrong with Fred's effort? It's too long, too complicated, and too fuzzy to sufficiently narrow his focus. He may want to include all the points he's listed. But he hasn't yet found his main idea.

Fred makes another stab at it. "My main point is that everyone ought to buy in on this new plan." Better. Now Fred is getting more concise. But he has focused on what he wants from the audience (the second crucial step, as you will see shortly). Instead, he initially needs to focus on what he wants to communicate.

So Fred tries again. "My main point is that the new marketing plan…" The words sit there on the page, staring back, challenging him to write more. He tries to clear his mind. "What is it I really want to say to the group?" he asks himself. "What's the one single thing that's most important for them to hear?"

And then, suddenly, it's clear. "What I really want to say is that this new marketing plan is a winner!"

There. Now Fred has a handle on his presentation. He has some clarity and focus. He now has a central idea around which he can organize everything else he needs to present. The main point becomes the stack-pole that helps organize the rest of the presentation.

Complete Exercise #5 to try your hand at finding the main idea.

"You've got to be very careful if you don't know where you are going, because you might get there."
—Yogi Bera

Exercise #5:

Finding the Main Point

Without rereading or looking back over what you just read, what would you say is the main point of this chapter so far? Write it out in your own words in one simple declarative sentence.

_____

_____

_____

Now check yourself. Look back over the preceding section and see if you accurately captured the key idea.

Writing Your Theme Statement

A written statement of your main point is sometimes called a *theme statement*. To be useful, a theme statement needs to be BASIC.

Brief—Keep it to one or two sentences at most.

Acute—Make it sharp and to the point.

Specific—Use concrete words, not abstractions and generalities.

Idea-Focused—Name the main idea you want to communicate.

Concise—Focus on one clear, concise idea.

While it's tempting to skip this step and simply begin to outline your presentation, disciplining yourself to write out a theme statement is well worthwhile. Like planning a project, investing a few minutes in writing a theme statement at the front-end of preparing a presentation can pay big dividends down the road.

Here are some benefits of having a written theme statement:

- Clarifies your thinking
- Chases away the fuzzies and foggies
- Provides a central, organizing idea for the rest of the presentation
- Speeds the overall process of putting a presentation together
- Gives you a way to sift necessary from unnecessary material
- Improves the chance the audience will get your key point
- Disciplines and trains your mind to be concrete and specific
- Diminishes the stress of preparing and organizing
- Yields better presentations which, in turn, makes you more promotable and visible

Apply It Now!

Write a Theme Statement

Think about the case study presentation you identified in Chapter 1. Ask yourself these questions:

1. What's the main thing you want to say?

   _____

   _____

2. What's the main point you hope to communicate?

   _____

   _____

3. What's the most important thing you want your listeners to remember?

   _____

   _____

4. If you had only one minute to make your presentation, what would you say?

   _____

   _____

5. Now, write out your own theme statement:

   _____

   _____

Next, use the BASIC definition to evaluate the theme statement you just wrote:

Brief—Is it one or two sentences at most?

Acute—Is it sharp and to the point?

Specific—Did you use concrete words rather than abstractions and generalities?

Idea-Focused—Does it name the main idea you want to communicate?

Concise—Does it identify one clear, concise idea?

If your theme statement falls short of these criteria, rewrite it. Remember, the time you spend now on writing a good theme statement will save preparation time later.

To be an effective presenter, you must clearly answer the content question. But, as mentioned earlier, that's only half the process involved in narrowing your focus. The other half has to do with the impact you want to have on your audience.

Presenting for Change

Do you want to be able to present with power and effectiveness? Do you want to have something to say? If so, then you'll need to answer this question: *How are you asking your audience to change?*

"Wait just a moment," you might say. "Not every presentation is a call to action is it? Sometimes isn't the goal simply to inform?"

The answer is "yes" and "yes." Yes, every presentation is, or at least ought to be, a call to action. And, yes, sometimes the goal is simply to inform. But to give people information they have previously lacked is to ask for a change—a change of perception, of mind, or of attitude.

You are accustomed to persuasive speech. It bombards you from all sides and through every available conduit. "Change long-distance companies." "Buy Brand X." "Vote for our candidate." But some presenters aren't used to thinking of their own presentations as attempts to get an audience to change— and that's why many presentations seem rather lifeless and arid! What about you? Are you presenting for change? Are you intent on impacting your audience in a way that requires a response from them? Do you see yourself as a change catalyst when you present?

Consider this: If you aren't asking your audience to change in some way—either in their actions, attitudes, understanding, perceptions, opinions, or plans, then why are you bothering to address them?

The presentation that doesn't seek to change is probably a presentation that isn't worth presenting. Having something to say means having something that will somehow affect your audience, that will make a difference to them.

Not every presentation needs to be a call to revolution, an earth-shaking announcement, or a life-changing inspiration. In fact, you very seldom encounter such information, much less have the opportunity to present it.

But even the most routine presentation can effect change. Consider a project update, for example. Depending on the information you present, you might be asking your audience to celebrate, redouble their efforts, revise their plans, make new decisions, or look for new jobs!

How about Fred's presentation? His main point, you remember, is that the new marketing plan is a winner. So what will he ask of his audience? What change might he seek?

Perhaps he'll ask his audience to lend their wholehearted support to the plan. Maybe he'll ask them to pick holes in it so he can make it even better. Or maybe he simply wants them to have the information they'll need to adjust to the coming changes.

In any case, his presentation will be far stronger if he is clear in his own mind about the impact he wants to make.

Writing a Purpose Statement

The theme statement focuses on content, but the purpose statement focuses on the specific impact you want to have on your audience. Begin by asking yourself these kinds of questions:

- What new information, if any, are you presenting?

- What do you want your listeners to do with this information?

- In light of your main point, what action would you like to see people take?

- What change in perception or understanding are you seeking to make?

- What specific actions or changes in behavior are you asking your audience to make?

- If there isn't a specific behavioral change you're asking for, is there an attitudinal change you're aiming at?

- If your presentation could do all you hope it could do, your audience would... (finish this sentence).

Writing out your answers to these kinds of questions helps you achieve a clear, focused, and specific presentation. The Apply It Now! exercise on the next page gives you an opportunity to practice writing a purpose statement.

Remember, the goal at this stage of preparation is to simply narrow your focus, to understand clearly what you want to accomplish in the presentation. The next stage will be gathering the necessary material and information. Still later will come the process of ordering the material and breathing life into it. But for now, the most important step is knowing where you are headed—knowing not only the main thing you want to say, but also the impact you want to have. After you have gathered more material and completed more research, you may want to change your focus. That's okay. Simply rewrite your theme statement and purpose statement in light of your new perspective.

Apply It Now!
Write a Purpose Statement

Think about the case study presentation you identified in
Chapter 1.

1. How do you want to impact your audience's actions,
   thoughts, feelings, attitudes?

   _____

   _____

2. Write out you own purpose statement, responding to this
   question: *How are you asking your audience to change?*

   _____

   _____

3. Evaluate it.

   • Is it brief and to the point?

   • Is it action-focused? Does it name the specific action or
   response you will be asking for?

   • Is this a change you have made and embraced yourself?
   (Remember, people pay more attention to your deeds than
   to your words.)

When This Approach Won't Work

Almost always it's best to begin with your purpose in mind. But sometimes this won't work. Sometimes you really don't know which direction a presentation should take until you've gathered more data, done more research, read more widely, or simply let it simmer a while. In those instances, it's best to go ahead and plunge into the gathering of your material, keeping the two key questions in mind. Then, after you have delved into your material, go back and apply the principles of this chapter.

Key Idea Chart

1. To focus your presentation, you need to answer two key questions:

    • What is your main point?

    _____

    _____

    • How are you asking your audience to change?

    _____

    _____

2. It is very important that you write out your answers to these questions.

3. Your theme and purpose statements should be brief and to the point.

4. You will be at your most powerful when you present for change.

5. Write out below the key idea you got for yourself from Chapter 3.

_____

_____

_____

_____

Chapter Four

Gathering and Organizing Your Material

Think of a building that inspires, impresses, or intrigues you. Perhaps it's a skyscraper, a hotel, a church, or a private residence. What is it that distinguishes this structure from the surrounding buildings? What about it not only catches the eye, but also captivates the imagination and spirit? Why do some buildings intrigue, others inspire, and still others enrage? Underlying most great architecture is a wedding of the practical and the poetic—of functionality and fantasy.

A quality presentation is like that. It blends elements of artistic creation with the craftsman-like skills of construction. On the one hand, you need a plan, a pattern, a blueprint. These are foundations you use to build on. They provide a system for bringing the various components together into a unified whole. On the other hand, if your presentation is to be effective, it has to have something of you in it—some life, color, uniqueness, and creativity.

In this chapter, you will learn how to gather and organize the raw materials of your presentation. You'll learn some systematic ways to go about assembling your raw materials into a coherent structure with definition and shape. But every presenter is unique and every presentation is an original creation. So you'll also learn some ways to bring your own creativity and color to bear upon the process.

Sources and Resources for Your Presentation

The United Way kickoff meeting occurs every year—it's as predictable as clockwork. But it's taken on new significance for Shawna ever since she was assigned the job of being the keynote speaker, which entails a twenty-minute presentation. The committee was unanimous. She had the experience, the abilities, and the enthusiasm to fire up the other campaign workers and help the company reach, if not exceed, its United Way goal. The only problem was, Shawna wasn't at all sure what she wanted to say.

Fortunately, she got the assignment a couple of months in advance. After giving it a great deal of thought, she wrote out a theme statement. "I want to explain why this drive is vital, not just to our community, but to our company and to the individual workers." She also thought through her purpose statement. "I want not only to explain, but also to inspire. I want the United Way team to make a real commitment to this campaign and to launch their efforts full of enthusiasm and confidence."

So far, so good. She knew where she was going. But how to get there? Twenty minutes for a presentation may not seem like much time. But it's an eternity if you don't know what you're going to say. Shawna wondered where she was going to get the "stuff" of her presentation—the meat that would flesh out her talk.

Every presenter faces the challenge of gathering, sorting, organizing, and making sense of the material that will make up the presentation. The kind of material to be gathered varies greatly according to the kind of presentation you will be making. A quarterly budget or accounting presentation will certainly demand a different set of information than Shawna's keynote address. But even the most highly technical or scientific presentation becomes easier to listen to and comprehend when the presenter puts a human face on the data. Conversely, a motivational or inspirational talk is bolstered by solid statistics or corroborating evidence.

So where do you go when it's time for the hard work of gathering your material for a presentation? The resources are plentiful.

Gather As You Go

Usually when you're researching a topic, you're more limited by time than by availability. The pressure of the deadline prevents many speakers from doing as thorough and adequate a job of research as they'd prefer. That's one reason those who present regularly get in the habit of gathering potentially useful material about the topics they present on as they go along.

"A story should have a beginning, a middle, and an end... but not necessarily in that order."
—Jean Luc Goddard

Fortunately for Shawna, she had just such a file. Ever since she'd volunteered for the United Way task force the previous year, she'd been saving articles, anecdotes, newspaper clippings, and various other information that related to the campaign. So the first thing she did when faced with the keynote address was get out her file and see what she already had.

If you have to make presentations regularly as a part of your profession or job, get in the habit now of gathering material as you go along. You don't have to wait until you have a particular speaking assignment to start collecting pertinent material. If you hear a good story or joke, write it down. If you read an informative article in a professional journal about your area of work, rip it out and file it. If you hear another speaker presenting on a topic you're interested in, take notes. A good guideline to remember is this: It's always better to have too much material and have to winnow it, than to have too little material.

That Venerable Institution: The Brainstorm

But what if you don't have a file like Shawna's? What if you're starting from scratch?

One of the best places to begin your search for relevant material for your presentation is right inside your own head! Before you read what others might have to say on your topic, before you consult the experts, before you research the media or the masses, dip deeply into the well of your own experience, creativity, and accumulated wisdom. You may be surprised at the reservoir of good ideas quietly residing there.

That old standby technique, brainstorming, is a good way to begin. Without censoring or prejudging the relevance or value of your ideas, just list out what you already know about your topic. Write down key ideas, words, phrases, facts, stories, and so on that come to mind. Discard nothing. What may appear at first glance to be unrelated to your subject may tie in later. Remember, at this point you are gathering material. There will be time enough later to sort it. (If there's not time, you'll know to start the preparation process sooner next time!)

The fact is, you probably already know a great deal about the subject of your presentation or you wouldn't have been selected as the speaker. So don't discount your own wealth of information, experience, and creativity. Let your brain storm—and catch what falls out. Once you have your own ideas down on paper (or in the word processor), it's time to broaden your research.

Other Information Sources

The information needed to fashion some business presentations is already at hand—reports, memos, budgets, specification sheets, project notebooks, market research data, and so forth. Other presentations will require more extensive research. The more you know about your topic, the easier it will be to zero in on the most important information to include in your presentation. And the more you know, the more confidently you'll present. Where do you go to get more information, usable illustrations, and, hopefully, a spark of inspiration? The sources are almost limitless. The accompanying "ABCs" chart provides a number of common as well as out-of-the ordinary resources.

"Don't agonize, organize."
—Jonathan Clark

The ABCs of Presentation Resources and Materials

A   Articles, archives, abstracts, atlases, allies, audits, authorities

B   Books, biographies, business journals, bathroom graffiti, the Bible

C   Cards, case studies, celebrities, CNN, comedy clubs, conversations, correspondence

D   Databases, daydreams, departmental memos, declarations

E   E-mail, eavesdropping, educators, editorials, employees, encyclopedias

F   Financial pages, fiction, fables, family, friends, faxes, forecasts

G   Government reports, gatherings, gossip, gadflies, gazettes, goals

H   Headlines, hallways, hairdressers, handouts, headquarters

I   Interviews, indexes, illustrations, insiders, imagination, indicators

J   Journals, jesters, jottings, journalists, junk mail

K   Keynote addresses, killjoys, kingpins, knowledgeable folks

L   Libraries, lab reports, laptops, lectures, letters, lexicons, literature

M	Magazines, mentors, movies, managers, MTV, mission statements
N	Networking, newspapers, NPR, nature, neighbors, novels
O	Op/Ed page, owners, orators, oldsters, officials, observations
P	Poetry, pop culture, public television, periodicals, proceedings, pictures, polls
Q	Quips, quotations, questionnaires
R	Research reports, radio, raconteurs, recollections, referrals, reviews
S	Songs, speeches, surveys, samples, scholars, Shakespeare, seminars, stories
T	Table talk, television, tabloids, theater, thesaurus
U	Unabridged dictionaries, unimpeachable sources, university studies
V	Valedictorians, vendors, various viewpoints, videos, vital speeches
W	Well-known persons, whodunits, windbags, wisecracks, workbooks
X	Xeroxed reports, X-rays
Y	Yearbooks, yourself, youngsters
Z	Zingers, zany folks, zealots

As you can see from the chart, the resources available are limited only by your imagination and the time you have to gather data. You will likely find professional journals, books, and interviews the most fruitful to explore at first. But don't discount casual conversations and popular culture, especially as a rich resource for illustrations. If, in your searching, you come across some interesting facts, a winsome story, or a memorable quote, don't forget your ideas and illustrations file. If the material isn't useful for this particular presentation, it may well come in handy for the next one.

You can use the Appy It Now! exercise on the next page to get started planning your research.

"This comes up all the time in mechanical work. A hang-up. You sit and stare and think, and search randomly for new information, and go away and come back again, and after awhile the unseen factors start to emerge."

—Robert M. Pirsig, *Zen and the Art of Motorcycle Maintenance*

Apply It Now!

Plan Your Research

Think about the case study presentation you identified in Chapter 1.

1. List the resources you already have on hand that you can use to help you prepare:

   _____

   _____

   _____

   _____

2. Now, list four specific sources you could turn to for additional information, illustrations, and details:

   _____

   _____

   _____

   _____

3. Set a deadline for completing your research:

   _____

Simmer Time and the Living Is Easy

After Shawna consulted the file she'd been compiling, she realized she needed to do some more research. Keeping the motivational purpose of her presentation in mind, she called the national United Way office to request some materials. Then she went to the library to do some browsing, copying, and information gathering. Within a couple of weeks, she had assimilated an amazing amount of information, read it all, and taken copious notes.

The task of sifting the important from the unimportant and then assembling the various pieces into a coherent presentation loomed on the horizon. But before Shawna plunged into that task, she took time for a step many inexperienced presenters often overlook. She did nothing. She let things simmer!

One of the reasons you'll want to start preparing your presentation as early as possible is to allow time for this vital step. Your subconscious is one of your most powerful tools for preparing presentations. Give it time to work. The subconscious mind is amazing in its ability to make connections between seemingly disparate elements, to sift and sort, to arrange and rearrange, to seek patterns and solve problems. Creativity can't be forced, and while some people can be amazingly productive when backed up against a deadline, most people do well to let their ideas gestate. Work a bit and rest a bit. Read over your material and then get away from it for awhile. Let it simmer.

Exercise #6:

Tuning In to Your Creativity

When and where do you get your most creative ideas? in the shower? while driving? while sleeping? late at night? early in the morning?

For the next week, pay attention to the moments when creative ideas hit you. Use the space below to record the time of day, what you were doing, and what the idea is. Do you see any patterns emerging that help you identify your peak creative place and time? If so, why do you think ideas seem to come to you then? Do you have a method for capturing them when they come? Don't rely on memory. Write them down or record them on tape.

Time of Day   **Activity**   **Idea**

_____   _____   _____

_____   _____   _____

_____   _____   _____

_____   _____   _____

_____   _____   _____

_____   _____   _____

55

The Possible Points List

After you've given your research a chance to cook a while, it's time to begin shaping your presentation. There's nothing particularly easy about this stage of preparation. It requires discipline and, preferably, an uninterrupted hour or two. Look back over the material you've gathered and the notes you've taken. Then list all the possible points you could make during your presentation. Once again, use the brainstorming technique. Don't evaluate ideas. Simply list them.

Shawna's list looked like this:

1. The United Way helps a lot of people.

2. Some of our own employees and their families benefit.

3. Everyone who donates benefits:

   • We get good feelings.

   • It builds morale.

   • We never know when we'll be the ones needing help.

4. It's good for the company (in terms of PR).

5. Our goal is a stretch, but it's reachable.

6. You (the UW team) are the backbone of the whole thing—it's up to you.

Apply It Now!

Make Your Possible Points List

Think about the case study presentation you identified in Chapter 1. Make a list of the possible points you could make during your presentation.

1. _____
2. _____
3. _____
4. _____
5. _____
6. _____
7. _____
8. _____
9. _____
10. _____

Distill Your Key Points

Now that Shawna had her possible points list, it was time to distill it. She had done enough public speaking to know that she shouldn't try to make too many points. She thought back to her theme statement: "I want to explain why this drive is vital, not just to our community, but to our company and the individual workers." She also thought about her purpose—to inspire and call for commitment, not just inform. With these big picture considerations in mind, she set about the task of sifting and narrowing down her possible points list to the most important two or three ideas.

How many points should you try to make in a presentation? It depends a great deal upon the kind of presentation you are making. In a detailed financial report or technical presentation, you may need to make a considerable number of points to cover the necessary information, whereas one point may be enough for an inspirational or motivational presentation.

As a general guideline, however, most presentations should have one clear and overriding theme, supported or expanded upon in no more than three subpoints. Long lists of points can get deadly boring. The old oration guideline, "Three points and a poem," contained some wisdom. Three clear points, well-illustrated and presented with intelligence, humor, and appropriate passion is a full serving for most audiences. If it's necessary for you to present a number of points and subpoints, then you'll want to be sure to supplement your verbal presentation with handouts or other visual aids (see Chapter 5).

How do you decide which of your possible points to use? Go back to your theme and purpose statements. Which of the points on your Possible Points list most directly and immediately support your overall theme and purpose? Another consideration is, of course, your audience's needs. What points would be most important to them and most connect with their needs? You might also ask yourself which points touch your personal convictions or investments. Those points are likely to be ones you would communicate well. Again, depending on the nature of the presentation, one other factor to consider is the illustrations you've gathered. If you're undecided between two points, go with the one that you're able to support with a good story, quote, or statistic.

Having weighed these factors, Shawna decided on these points:

1. The United Way helps a lot of people and does a lot of good.

2. Everyone who donates benefits:

   • We get good feelings.

   • It builds morale.

   • We never know when we'll be the ones needing help.

3. It's good for the company (in terms of PR).

Apply It Now!

Key Points List

Look over your Possible Points list, keeping in mind the case study you chose in Chapter 1. Think about your overall theme and purpose, your audience's needs, your own commitments, and potential illustrations. Now, list no more than two or three key points you want to make.

1. _____

   _____

   _____

   _____

2. _____

   _____

   _____

   _____

3. _____

   _____

   _____

   _____

Organize and Outline

Once you've narrowed your focus to a few key points, it's time to arrange and organize your material. There are a number of different ways you can arrange your points so you can develop them clearly and make it easy for your audience to follow your presentation.

One approach is to look for a natural or logical progression of thought. If one idea or point flows naturally out of another, then you have a ready-made sequence to follow. A logical arrangement of your ideas makes transitions easier and helps your audience follow your line of thinking (see Chapter 8).

Another option is to arrange your points in order of importance. Usually you will want to move from the least important to the most important idea, but there may be occasions when you want to lead off with your most important point. For example, if you have a presentation to make to a client and you're afraid she may get interrupted or called away abruptly, then you would want to make your key point first.

Arranging your points to build emotional intensity is another way to organize your presentation. Again, the usual pattern would be to build towards a powerful ending, saving your most forceful point to last.

Some presenters use a "circle the wagons" kind of organization. This is useful when you have one key idea that you want to drive home in a variety of ways. You state your key idea and then keep circling back to it as you make each subpoint.

Mnemonic devices such as acronyms and alliteration also offer useful patterns of arrangement. These can be very helpful to presenters and speakers alike because they are so memorable. The danger is they can rather easily become overly artificial, strained, or cute.

Whatever tool you settle on, the key is to order your main points in such a way that you feel confident about your material. The whole point of this step of preparation is to help you (and later your audience) get a handle on the information so you can arrange (and they can grasp it) in a way that makes sense.

As Shawna looked over her key points, she let her mind experiment with different arrangements. Remembering the KISS rule of presenting (Keep It Short and Simple), Shawna fine-tuned her key points until she came up with this outline:

You can wholeheartedly solicit for the United Way because:

1. It helps our community.

2. It helps our company.

3. It helps your co-workers and you.

What had previously been a pile of documents, research, and random ideas was now beginning to take shape as a meaningful presentation. Soon Shawna would be ready for the next step, adding life and color.

Apply It Now!
Organize and Outline

In regard to the case study you chose in Chapter 1, look over your key points. Experiment with different ways to sequence them. Find a way that works for you and outline it below.

_____

_____

_____

_____

_____

_____

_____

_____

_____

_____

_____

_____

_____

Key Idea Chart

1. A very valuable resource in preparing your presentation is your own creativity and knowledge.

2. Don't be selective when you begin gathering material.

3. When you're planning a presentation, it's important to build in time to let your ideas simmer.

4. A very useful step is to create a Possible Points list.

5. As a general rule, it's best not to have more than three key points.

6. There are several ways to arrange and organize your material.

7. Write out below the key idea you got from Chapter 4.

_____

_____

_____

_____

_____

_____

_____

_____

_____

Chapter Five

Bringing Your Presentation to Life

The first goal of any presenter is to be listened to. Otherwise, what's the point? You may have wonderful ideas, impeccable credentials, flawless logic, unimpeachable research, and a heart of gold, but if people tune you out, you've lost the battle—if not the war. You can't sell your product, enlist your client, close your deal, inspire your employees, or have your solutions accepted if your listeners quit listening. It's not enough to identify your key points and arrange them in a clear, communicable sequence. You must also find a way to hold your audience's interest and attention.

This is where the *art* of presenting comes in—the hallmark of a crafty presenter is being able to breathe life into a presentation. Adding vitality and color to your presentation requires some artistry, creativity, risk taking, and experimenting. There's a world of difference between a boring talk and a lively one. And the difference is this: The lively one gets listened to. The boring one gets ignored. How can you animate your presentation so people will not only listen to you, but remember what you've said?

In this chapter, you'll look at six powerful ways to accomplish this:

1. Personal investment in your topic

2. The variety and value of illustrations

3. The power of the personal

4. The effectiveness of humor

5. The importance of pacing

6. The impact of the visual

Personal Involvement in Your Topic

Dale Carnegie said, "A person under the influence of his feelings, projects the real self, acting naturally and spontaneously. A speaker who is interested will usually be interesting."

Do you believe in what you are presenting? Do you personally find it interesting? Do you have a stake in it? Have you taken the trouble to get inside your subject and really understand it? Do you have something you believe is worth other people hearing?

"Generally, audiences want to laugh, rally behind a cause, listen to stories, enjoy themselves—and feel something."

—Roger Ailes (Speech consultant to President Bush)

The simple fact is this: You will present more effectively if you believe in what you're saying. This truth is most obvious in certain kinds of presentations—sales presentations, motivational and inspirational talks, and persuasive speeches. In these instances, especially, you're not just selling your ideas; you're also selling yourself. The absence or presence of conviction, sincerity, and integrity can make all the difference between a successful presentation and one that falls flat.

But many business presentations don't fit these categories. In fact, many, if not most presentations in business settings are more informational in nature. Even so, if you want to present powerfully and effectively, you will need to take the time to tune into your subject and invest in it personally—at least to some extent. An old axiom of presenting is this: "Get inside your subject. Then get your subject inside of you. Then, you'll have a chance to get it inside your audience."

Jim is making a presentation to management on the results of his team's research into new computer networking software options. Although he has a great deal of data and recommendations to offer, he also has firsthand experience with the problems the old system created and has talked to the front-line workers who were most affected. He's heard their complaints and suggestions and knows that the present system is hurting productivity and morale. He understands that what's at stake isn't just software; it's also the welfare of his fellow employees. Consequently, he brings some conviction to his presentation. He's invested enough in the subject to be not only knowledgeable, but also concerned.

One important point about conviction: it isn't easily quantified. You can enumerate your illustrations. You can tally your visual aids. You can list your stories. But you can't count your conviction. What you can count on, however, is this: the absence of conviction will definitely weaken your presentation.

How do you show conviction? There are two important ingredients. One is to do your homework thoroughly. The more you know about your subject, the more you've read, researched, reflected, and ruminated, the more likely you are to develop some personal investment in your material. There's usually a lot of digging to be done to find a diamond. Dig into your subject and you're far more likely to find a gem. Remember, you have to get inside your material before you can get it inside of you.

Second, always ask the human connection questions:

- What relevance does this material have for me personally?

- What beliefs, assumptions, prejudices, or biases of mine does this material stir up?

- What stake do I have in the outcome of this presentation?

- How does this information touch on the concerns or needs of my audience?

- What difference could this material make to people's lives?

- What needs am I addressing?

- What feelings or beliefs would this subject intersect with for most people?

- So what?

It's important to ask these questions as you prepare because you can be sure your audience will be asking them as you present. Some presentations simply aren't much laden with the cargo of human freight. But many are, and to the extent you can add feeling to facts, depth to data, or heart to head, you will add interest to your presentation.

Complete Exercise #7 on the next page to begin building your expertise in using your personal belief in your topic to capture the interest and attention of your audience.

"Let us have reason for beginning and let our end be within due limits. For a speech that is wearisome only stirs up anger."

—St. Ambrose, Bishop of Milan, 4th century A.D.

Exercise #7:

Making It Personal

Pick a news article at random from a magazine or newspaper. Ask of it the human connection questions. Does the article answer or address these? If not, what relevance, stake, or connection can you find between the article and your life?

_____

_____

_____

_____

_____

_____

_____

_____

_____

The Value and Variety of Illustrations

Once upon a time there was a young woman named Samantha. Samantha wanted to succeed. She wanted to do well in her job, move ahead in her career and, in general, win friends and influence people. Samantha had studied hard in graduate school, landed a great starting position, and moved forward in a deliberate and measured way. She was all set to prosper.

But then she advanced to a new position in which she had to make frequent presentations. Samantha would research thoroughly, prepare well in advance, and even practice her presentations in front of Miss Merriweather, her cat. But to no avail. She was boring. She knew her stuff. But as soon as she began to speak, the sandman would sprinkle his dust about the room. Eyes would glaze over, heads would nod, and Samantha would find herself presenting to the walls.

Then one day, while baby-sitting her four-year-old nephew, Winston, she had a revelation. Winston had asked her to read him the story of the "Three Pigs and the Inside Trader" for the fifteenth time. It was as if her ears were hearing, for the very first time in her life, those magic words, "once upon a time." And so it was that Samantha learned the power of a story and began to include them in her presentations. She soon was promoted again, pursued by many suitors, bought a BMW, and lived happily ever after. The end.

Have you learned yet the power of a story? They may not gain you suitors and a BMW, but they can help you make better presentations and promote your career. Illustrations are the soul of a presentation. They breathe life into what would otherwise be no more than a skeleton of an outline, a listless body of information, a corpse of dry data. Does this mean you must become a great raconteur to succeed at presenting? No, not at all. But it does mean that you neglect the art of illustrating your presentation at great peril. Salespeople know that what sells isn't so much the steak as it is the sizzle, and good presenters know that what holds an audience's attention isn't simply good data, but data presented in a lively, interesting and, best of all, entertaining fashion.

Why? No one knows for sure. Maybe it has to do with the fact that people are storytelling creatures and that stories give meaning and definition to human existence. Maybe it's because a story reconnects people to early nurturing experiences of being held in their parents' arms. Whatever the reasons, the fact is that illustrations can be very powerful.

Think back, for example, to a favorite childhood story. What do you remember about it? How do you feel when you recall it? Who read or told you this story? What does this say to you about the power of stories and illustrations?

The Value of Illustrations

Illustrations are valuable because they can do so many important things for your presentation. They can:

- Clarify your point.
- Elicit audience response.
- Hold people's attention.
- Lighten up a presentation.
- Touch the emotions.
- Help you pace your presentation.
- Serve as a transition between points.

- Add humor and good feelings.

- Make bad news more palatable.

- Make you a more powerful presenter.

John has been making a persuasive case for his client to change his advertising strategy. The old advertising approach has been producing declining results for several months. Nonetheless, the client seems reluctant to risk a change. John has presented research data about the new strategy from focus groups and a sampling survey. He has numbers, names, and notations. But the client doesn't seem to be budging.

So John illustrates his point. "Mr. Marken, last Saturday I took my son to see the circus. We were both entranced by the trapeze artists. What was especially exciting was when the moment came for the artist to let go of one bar and turn around in mid-air, trusting that the new bar would be there to grab hold of. Of course, it wasn't blind luck. They had practiced and prepared, just like we have in proposing this new concept. But still, the moment came when the artist had to risk letting go and turning around, trusting and hoping that the bar would be there. I don't blame you for being hesitant about this change we've been discussing. You and I both know how competitive this industry has become, not to mention the fact that the safety net isn't very big anymore. But I honestly believe you're at the point where you need to let go and risk it. If not, you'll just keep on swinging on the same old bar until the company loses momentum. It's your decision, of course, but I think it's a risk worth taking. What more information do you need to be able to let go of that bar?"

John's illustration, drawn from a field totally unrelated to the business at hand, made bright his client's dilemma and the imperative nature of his decision. It focused the discussion on the crucial issue, put all the data into relative perspective, and pressed for a decision. The best stories not only illuminate, they also demand of the listener or reader some kind of verdict. Agreement or disagreement? Innocence or guilt? Trust or doubt? Buy or don't buy? Action or inaction?

Paradoxically, illustrations can also "lighten up" a presentation. There are very few situations or occasions for a presentation that wouldn't profit from a bit of levity or humor. These kinds of breaks in the intensity of a presentation help the audience stay tuned in and alert. They recapture the wandering mind and energize both the audience and the speaker.

Illustrations also have the power to touch the emotions in a way that factual information simply can't. A good business presentation, as you have seen, must make sense. It must be supported by logic, facts, details, and reliable data, all reasonably interpreted. But the most powerful presentations speak to the heart as well as to the head. They appeal to the emotions, not just to the mind. Stories and examples that cause people to laugh and to feel anger, sadness, or wonder can be extremely effective when they support solid research and sound thinking.

Complete Exercise #8 to examine how professional advertisers use illustrations in relation to text to appeal to the reader's emotions.

Exercise #8:

Appealing to Emotions

Open a magazine and look over the advertising. Study it as a prime example of persuasive speech. What portion of most ads relies on text, data, facts, information?

_____

_____

_____

What portion aims at the emotions, heart, impulses? Which speaks the most to you? Why?

_____

_____

_____

_____

_____

_____

Data gets dull. Illustrations add interest. They break the pace and can add a much-needed element of humor or laughter. They can serve as bridges between the various points of your presentation. They can even help when your presentation requires you to deliver bad news. Of course, you want to deliver the bad news up front in a clear and straightforward fashion. It does no good to hide it or sugarcoat it. But an illustration showing that you understand the concrete impact of the news on the people affected may soften the blow.

There is, of course, no substitute for hard facts, thorough research, reasoned conclusions, and careful analysis. The first requirement is for you to have something to say. But illustrations can make the difference between your message being heard and being ignored, between being a so-so presenter and being a powerful presenter. Experiment with the great variety of ways you can illustrate your presentation, and be attuned to the impact your illustrations have on your audience.

Varieties of Illustrations

There are a variety of ways you can illustrate your presentation. You can use examples, analogies, comparisons or contrasts, object lessons, anecdotes and stories, and other techniques. What all of these have in common is the power to clarify.

Consider the root of the word "illustration." It comes from the Latin *illustrare,* meaning "to make bright." That's exactly what an aptly chosen illustration does. It makes bright. It sheds light upon. It clarifies. A presentation can become dense and dark with data, information, logic, and arguments. An illustration illuminates that density and lets an audience see the point more clearly.

Examples. Examples are often useful in business presentations. When you illustrate with an example, you pick out one particular instance or case that is representative of or serves as a model or pattern for the point you're making. For example, Sue is touting the benefits of a new software package to her work team. Having explained some of its key features, she zeroes in on one particular application and shows the team members exactly how the new software would handle that problem. She illustrates her overall point—the value of the new program—by means of one particular aspect of it.

Examples help make the points of your presentation concrete and specific. The educational and philosophical tradition of the Western world tends towards abstractions and generalizations. In the East, the opposite is true. There, stories, proverbs, and concrete examples are the main teaching mode. In the West, we might say, "The adolescent who lacks consistent discipline and adequate role modeling from a unified family unit will often demonstrate socially inappropriate behavior patterns, poor social bonding, diminished peer relationships, and susceptibility to acting out." Someone from the East might say, "If the father eats garlic and the mother eats onions, will not the son stink?"

Never hesitate to illustrate your presentation with an example that makes your general point specific. Doing so will not only help you communicate more clearly to your audience, it will also discipline you to think more concretely. Using this technique is also a good way to learn to anticipate the audience's questions, which tend to be more about specifics than generalities.

Analogies. Analogies rely on showing a correspondence between two things that are alike in certain respects, but are otherwise dissimilar. Using an analogy in a business presentation is like splashing color onto a black-and-white picture. It enlivens and catches your audience's interest and attention. Sue employed an analogy when she said, "This new software is like a Ferrari in a Ford body. It looks ordinary enough until you press on the accelerator, and then it takes off!" What makes this an analogy rather than a simple comparison is that software and automobiles are for the most part unrelated, yet Sue bridged the two.

Two techniques can increase the effectiveness of analogies. One is to draw analogies from the common, ordinary experiences of everyday life. Find analogies that anyone can relate to—analogies drawn from family life, daily business, or shared experiences the group has in common. (Remember, it's important to know your audience.) After all, the whole point of an analogy is to help your audience relate the concept or idea you are presenting to their lives and experiences. Consider this example: "At first, getting your client to even consider this idea is going to be like getting your kid to try spinach. They'll squirm, resist it, and say 'Yuck!' But if we can ever get them to try a bite, they'll find that not only is it good for them, it doesn't taste half bad."

A second thing to keep in mind is that the more dissimilar the two things you're comparing are, the more powerful the analogy will probably be. "Meeting our deadline on this project is like getting the budget in on time" isn't nearly as effective as this: "OK, team, it's the fourth down on this project and we're only two yards from the goal line. Complete this last crucial play and the game is ours!"

Exercise #9:

Create Some Analogies

Try your hand at creating some analogies. Read down the list in the left-hand column and draw a line connecting each one to something in the right-hand column.

IS LIKE

Drawing up a new budget	Hitting your head against a wall
Hiring a new employee	Batting .1000—it doesn't happen!
Getting the boss to level with you	Giving birth to a baby
Dealing with interruptions	Discovering a sunken treasure
Responding to customer complaints	Pulling teeth
Finding good service	Falling into quicksand
Completing everything on time	Falling off a log
Talking with my spouse	(Create your own)

————————————————

————————————————

————————————————

Comparisons and contrasts. Other useful tools you will want to keep on hand in your illustration toolbox are comparisons and contrasts. These tools function a lot like an analogy. They draw a comparison between two similar things or highlight how two things are different.

> *"Now, you don't need to get too anxious. This is a whole lot like what we went through in renegotiating the Miller contract. You remember how we..."*

> *"In contrast to the changes in production procedures last year, this revision will be a snap. It's nothing or, at least, next to nothing!"*

Comparisons and contrasts can be especially effective in persuasive presentations, when you want your clients to see how your service or product compares to their needs and also to contrast your proposal with what the competition offers.

Object lessons. If you think of object lessons as suitable only for children, you may be setting aside a powerful presentation tool. When you use an object lesson to illustrate, you present your audience with an actual object to look at. People may not remember all of your commentary, but you can be sure they'll go away remembering what you showed them.

Jan was doing some training for her department in cultural diversity in the workplace. After talking extensively about how diversity can enrich the workplace, but acknowledging that it stretches most people past their comfort zones, Jan unveiled her pièce de rèsistance—an apple pie, sopaipillas, and Chinese fortune cookies. Here was an object lesson that appealed to nearly all the senses—visual, smell, touch, and taste! You may not want to go to that much trouble, but do go to the trouble to consider how an object lesson might be a very powerful way to illustrate your next presentation. Use your own creativity.

Anecdotes and stories. Of all of the tools of illustration, anecdotes and stories may be the most powerful. Stories have a unique power to capture the imagination and emotions. They captivate interest, energize the audience, and forge a stronger bond between you and your listeners. Stories have the capacity to put a human face on facts and figures and to build a bridge from your presentation into the concerns of your customers, colleagues, and clients.

Where do you find suitable stories for your presentation? The resources are almost limitless. Storytelling is enjoying a renaissance these days and there are hundreds of anthologies available. Fables, anecdotes about famous people, character sketches, ethnic and regional stories, family and personal stories, biographies, mythology, classical literature and popular fiction, the movies, and, of course, your own imagination—all of these and many more are rich in story possibilities.

Like any illustration, a story needs to "fit" your presentation. Occasionally a speaker will begin with a story that is amusing or provoking, but has no real bearing on the presentation. Avoid this kind of artificiality. Remember, the goal is to make your presentation "bright"—to shed some light on your key points and to hold your audience's attention. So choose stories that clearly relate to your topic.

"Storytelling reveals meaning without committing the error of defining it."

—Hannah Arendt

In addition, avoid trite transitions such as "That reminds me of a story I once heard…" Instead, just proceed smoothly from your point into your story.

The way your story relates to your topic should be self-evident, requiring little or no explanation. A story you have to explain is not a suitable story. In fact, that's a good rule to use as you choose your stories. Ask yourself, "Does this story clearly connect to the point I'm trying to make, or will I need to explain its meaning or application for the audience?" If you feel you need to draw out the story's connection to your point, then you should probably discard that particular story. The whole point is that the story itself does the explaining. Another good question to ask yourself is, "Would this story stand on its own?" In other words, is it interesting in its own right? If not, discard it.

Melinda's work team was considering two options. She had been asked to research them and lead the team in reaching a decision. Having done her homework, Melinda knew that neither option was clearly superior to the other. Both had several pros and cons. The team was going to have to make a decision on something other than hard data. Melinda presented her research and her conclusion that neither direction was clearly better than the other. Then she concluded her presentation with a brief anecdote about a time she had been hiking in a national forest and had come to a fork in the trail. The map was very unclear. Both trails seemed to lead to the destination, but the decision itself came down to trusting her instinct. She embellished the story with a bit of detail, exaggeration, and color and then asked, "Which trail do your instincts tell you we should take?" Her story crystallized the situation and gave her work team a concrete image they could use to guide their decision making.

Brief anecdotes are like seasoning for a meal, adding spice and variety. Sprinkle them judiciously throughout your presentation. People love to hear about other people—their trials, failures, foibles, and successes. Periodicals such as *Guideposts* and *Reader's Digest* offer a wealth of these kinds of anecdotes. Their only drawback is that they are so widely read that some of your audience members will be familiar with your story.

Sometimes a story can serve as the stack-pole for your whole presentation. You begin the story, make one of your points, tell more of the story, make another point, and so on, until you conclude with the story's ending.

Rich was making a training presentation on the basics of project management. He introduced the topic by beginning to tell a true story about a particular construction project that went woefully astray. As he described the unfolding disaster, he made a variety of points about mistakes to avoid in project management. Then as he described how an experienced project manager salvaged the project, Rich was able to underscore several key ingredients to successful project management. The story not only served to illustrate his points about the pitfalls and priorities of project management, it also served as the stack-pole that united his presentation.

The Apply It Now! exercise on the next page will give you practice in developing your presentation by using anecdotes and stories.

Apply It Now!

Think of a Story

Think about the case study presentation you identified in Chapter 1 and one of the key points you know you want to make. Think of a brief anecdote or story that might illustrate this point. Write a brief summary of it below.

_____

_____

_____

_____

_____

_____

_____

_____

Evaluate your story's usefulness:

- Would it add human interest and color?

- Does it "fit" the point? Does it illuminate and make your point clearer?

- Is the point self-evident?

- Could it serve as an organizing tool for the presentation?

Examples, analogies, comparisons and contrasts, object lessons, and anecdotes and stories by no means exhaust your options to add color and life to your presentation. Case studies, quotations, statistics, lyrics, headlines, and your own creativity can expand your resources indefinitely. Of special importance are graphs, charts, overheads, and other visual aids. (These will be discussed later in the chapter). The essential thing is to find some appropriate illustrations. They add color, life, and interest to any presentation, increasing your likelihood of being heard.

The Power of the Personal

Is the personal element ever appropriate in a business presentation? Most certainly! In fact, it's not only appropriate, it's inevitable. Often you will be presenting *your* recommendations, the findings from *your* research, *your* analysis, *your* proposal, *your* plan, *your* project. Of course, the factual data must carry the weight. But your subjective judgments, opinions, and biases will inevitably color your presentations. The key is to be aware of these and use them deliberately as a tool. The only time they'll get you in trouble is when they are functioning outside your awareness. Beware of the presenter who thinks he or she is being totally objective and unbiased!

"If you think you are too small to be effective, you have never been in bed with a mosquito."

—Bethe Reese

Deliberately including a personal dimension in your presentation can have several positive effects. It can build a bridge between you and your audience. It can reassure your audience that you, too, bring personal considerations and questions to the issue at hand. It invites honesty and forthrightness in dialogue, discussion, and questioning. It rings of authenticity and sincerity. And it invites attention and careful listening.

The personal dimension can take many forms. It may mean using a personal anecdote or story to illustrate one of your points. Personal stories are riskier than third-party stories, but they are usually more powerful. After all, you're speaking about what you know best—your own life and experience.

Emil is training the customer service department in active listening skills. In addition to using several work-specific examples, he also shares a recent incident in which his failure to listen actively to his wife created confusion and tension. There is a murmur of recognition as he shares his story. Heads nod in acknowledgment, and Emil hears gentle laughter that says: "Yes, I've been there. I relate to that." Emil is no longer just a trainer speaking to trainees. He's now a fellow traveler who occasionally stumbles on the difficult road of human communication.

"The most instructive experiences are those of everyday life."
—Friedrich Nietzsche

Why is the personal touch so powerful? Because most people have a natural curiosity about others. And stories and illustrations that grow out of your everyday life provide your listeners with an instant point of recognition, contact, and empathy. They help you communicate with personal, not just positional, authority. Whether you're a CEO formally addressing your management team or the shop supervisor having a discussion with workers, the personal dimension communicates that not only is wisdom, authority, position, and power speaking, but also another human being who lives, sweats, succeeds, and fails just like everyone else.

Look around you. What's been happening in your family and social relationships? What's new with your hobbies and interests? Most people see themselves more clearly in mundane events rather than in momentous ones, in everyday occurrences rather than epoch-making events. That's not to say you shouldn't take advantage of the opportunity to use life's defining moments when they do occur and are relevant to your presentation. Talking about your daughter's birth in a way that illustrates your point is sure to get your audience's attention. But so can a simple story of dealing with your five-year-old who won't eat his peas. When preparing presentations, many people discount the value of their own experiences as a rich

"The man who writes about himself and his own time is the only man who writes about all people and all time."

—George Bernard Shaw

resource of examples and stories. One caution: If your illustration involves other family members, co-workers, or associates, be sure to get their permission before featuring them in your anecdote.

The other main way in which you can use the personal dimension to make your presentation better is to personalize your recommendations and conclusions. You can be sure every one of your listeners will be asking the WIIFM question: "What's In It For Me?" Answer this question personally. Let them know you have thought through not only what's in it for you, but also for them. This lets your audience know you are taking them seriously and have thought through your material carefully.

Apply It Now!

Identify the Personal Dimension of Your Presentation

Think about the case study presentation you identified in Chapter 1. Begin personalizing your presentation by •writing out your answers to these questions:

1. What personal stake do I have in the outcome of this presentation?

   _____

   _____

   _____

2. How have my life experiences influenced and colored the way I see the topic I'll be presenting?

   _____

   _____

   _____

3. What common personal stake do I share with my listeners in this presentation?

   _____

   _____

   _____

4. How could I illustrate my key ideas using my own life story or daily experience?

- Key point #1: _____

  Personal Illustration: _____

  _____

  _____

  _____

- Key point #2: _____

  Personal Illustration: _____

  _____

  _____

  _____

- Key point #3: _____

  Personal Illustration: _____

  _____

  _____

  _____

The Effectiveness of Humor

Of all the tools at your command to make your presentation come alive, none may be more potent than humor. How many times have you been listening to a presentation and found your attention wandering and your energy faltering only to be suddenly jarred back to alertness by a clever remark, funny story, or humorous comment? But humor does more than just catch people's interest. You can also use it to make your point powerfully.

A motivational speaker was talking about how difficulties can actually be tremendously enriching and growth-producing times for people. He wanted the audience to see that especially in times of darkness, there was potential for them to shine. So he told a true story about a camping trip he'd been on. The eight-year-old son of his hiking companions accidentally dropped a flashlight down the commode of an outhouse. Twelve feet below, it landed right-side up, faithfully shining its light up out of the toilet seat. In the dusk, as other campers came to the outhouse and opened the door, they were taken aback by the unearthly glow arising from the commode opening. Amidst the ensuing laughter, the speaker drove home his point. "No matter how deeply you've fallen into it, you can always find a way to let your light shine!" You can be sure his audience went home with a vivid image in their minds that sealed his point more powerfully than any somber lecture could have.

*"Good humor is a tonic for mind and body.
It is the best antidote for anxiety and
depression. It is a business asset."*

—Glenville Kleiser

But does humor have a place in business presentations? Most certainly! In his book *Learning to Laugh at Work* (SkillPath Publications, 1995), Robert McGraw argues persuasively that cultivating a sense of humor at work can help you polish your professional presence and win the respect of your co-workers. He makes the point that humor doesn't mean you don't take your job seriously enough, but rather that you don't take yourself too seriously. He also points out that, rightly used, humor can strengthen your sense of confidence, control, and authority and that most successful leaders evidence a strong, well-developed sense of humor.

If these observations are true of the workplace in general, how much more true are they when it comes to presentations! Nothing breathes life into a presentation and turns up the energy of an audience like a good laugh. "But," you say, "I'm just not a funny person. I can't even tell a good joke."

Not to worry! Just as you can improve the other skills of presenting, you can cultivate your sense of humor and increase your capacity to use this potent tool. You may not be a Bill Cosby, David Letterman, or Erma Bombeck. But you can become a person who uses humor naturally in your presentations.

In *Learning to Laugh at Work,* Robert McGraw offers a number of exercises you can use to improve your humor quotient. He invites readers to write down parody versions of familiar ads,

"The day most wholly lost is the one on which one does not laugh."

—Nicolas Chamfort

commercials, well-known songs, and famous people's names. He suggests turning clichés on their heads, offering this wonderful example: "He looked like something the cat refused to drag in." He recommends using the techniques of exaggeration and telling stories that personalize, localize, and allow the audience to empathize. As a presenter, be alert for opportunities to tailor your humor to the specific audience you're addressing.

Besides telling humorous stories, be alert for opportunities to tell a joke related to a point you're making. But don't feel like you must tell jokes. In fact, humor that grows out of your own life and situation is usually more potent than jokes that have been around for years. If you are going to use a joke, make sure it ties in clearly to your presentation and it's not offensive. Then, practice it to get the words and timing down.

Self-deprecating humor can be especially effective in putting an audience at ease. You will want to avoid putting yourself down in a way that communicates insecurity or appears to be an indirect request for affirmation. Rather, aim at humor that humanizes you before your audience and forges the bond of common recognition of life's absurdities. For instance, one bald-headed speaker made reference to a "hair-raising experience" he'd been through. Without missing a beat, he added, "Of course, as you can see, I had a crop failure!"

"What I want to do is make people laugh so they'll see things seriously."
—William K. Zinsser

Such humor is especially effective when things go awry. One presenter accidentally knocked his overhead projector, cart and all, off the platform, sending it crashing to the floor below. The audience got deathly quiet until the speaker slowly walked to the edge of the platform, peered down as if looking into a deep abyss, and then said, "Well, that's one way to get your attention!" From then on, he had their attention and their good will.

As you experiment with enlivening your presentations with humor, be sure to use good judgment. Will Rogers may have been right when he said, "Everything is funny as long as it is happening to somebody else," but when it comes to using humor in public speaking, make sure you don't target someone else in any way that could be construed as a put-down. Avoid all sexist humor, group stereotypes, and ethnic, racial, and religious humor. The only exception to this rule might be if you are a member of the group you're poking fun at and you're able to personalize the story. Another no-no, of course, is "off-color" or sexual humor, which not only risks offending, but is legally risky as well in light of the sensitivity to sexual harassment in today's workplace.

These exceptions aside, have fun! If humor doesn't come easily to you, get McGraw's book or other books on humor in the workplace and cultivate your funny bone. It can only enhance your professional standing, improve the quality of your presentations, and make you feel better. In the words of an ancient proverb, "A cheerful heart is good medicine, but a crushed spirit dries up the bones." Start now to infuse your presentations with the good medicine of a good laugh.

Try your hand at injecting humor into your presentations by completing the Apply It Now! exercise on the next page.

Apply It Now!
Add Humor to Your Presentation

Think about the presentation you identified in Chapter 1. Pick
out one of the key points you want to make and brainstorm
some ways you could breathe life into that point with humor.
In what ways might you:

Exaggerate?

_____

_____

Distort a cliché?

_____

_____

Relate a humorous personal anecdote?

_____

_____

Tell a joke?

_____

_____

Highlight an absurdity of everyday behavior?

_____

_____

The Importance of Pacing

Uniformity is the highest standard in some endeavors. In manufacturing, for instance, the goal is that every product off the line be exactly like its predecessor. But in presenting, uniformity becomes monotony and monotony becomes failure. Successful presentations are characterized by variety—of emphasis, vocal quality, intensity, and especially, pacing. Like distance runners, successful presenters know how to pace themselves.

Pacing has to do, primarily, with the *tempo* of your presentation, the speed at which you deliver your ideas. A slow, ponderous delivery quickly wearies even the most devoted listeners. Likewise, a breakneck, headlong rush through a presentation confounds, confuses, and fatigues your audience. Your best bet is to find your own natural pace—a rhythm of words and pauses that fits you. Then vary that natural pace for emphasis. You may want to use a rapid-fire delivery at certain points in a presentation to add needed emphasis and urgency. On the other hand, some points need time to sink in. An appropriately timed pause can catch your audience's attention as readily as a shout.

The key is to gauge your pace according to your audience's response. If you're picking up signals that things are dragging, then pick up the pace a bit. If your audience appears frazzled or confused, slow the pace down. As you vary your pace, also modulate the loudness and tone of your voice. Above all, avoid monotony.

"Sit, walk, or run, but don't wobble."

—Zen proverb

Notice the great variety in pace when different people talk. How does a five-year-old's pace differ from that of a fifty-five-year-old's? How does the emotional content of a message affect the pace of the person delivering it? Ask some friends to characterize your own pace of speech.

In addition to the actual speed of delivery, pace also refers to the *emotional intensity* of your delivery. If you've ever driven one of those arrow-straight interstate highways across big, flat, empty country, you know how boring the trip can quickly become. But a trip that includes peaks and valleys, turns and curves, dips and surprises keeps you awake and alert. Vary the emotional intensity of your presentational journey. Alternate between lightweight and heavyweight material. Move back and forth between clear reasoning and appeals to the emotions, between facts and fun, between head and heart. Humor, in particular, can be a good lead-in for a serious point. The humor softens the audience's defenses. Once you have them laughing, drive home a key idea.

The Impact of the Visual

"You've all been hearing many rumors about this year's sales incentive program, I know," Bob began. "And as usual, most of them aren't true!"

"After taking ninety-nine years to climb a stairway, the tortoise falls and says there is a curse on haste."

—Maltese proverb

Quiet, good-natured laughter shuffles across the room as the sales managers remember some of the outlandish ideas suggested in years past.

"No, the fact of the matter is," Bob continues, "what we've thought up this year is better than the rumors!" There is a slight stir of anticipation. "How would you like to have your choice of… "

Bob hesitates just a moment as he turns on the slide projector, displaying a shiny, brand new automobile. "This," he says, gesturing towards the car. "Or this," he gestures as the slide changes to a travel picture of Europe. "Or this?" he concludes, while showing a ski boat. Every eye is fixed on the screen and every mind attentive as Bob begins to unfold the details of the new incentive program. His sales managers may not remember every detail, but they won't soon forget that car, that vacation, or that boat.

"Look!" What a powerful word that is! In grade school primers of years gone by, it was one of the first words students learned. "Look. See Dick run. See Spot run." Reading education may have evolved over the years, but the power of the visual remains undiminished. Increasingly, learning has to do with looking and seeing as well as hearing. Indeed, televisions, computers, and other multimedia tools are becoming more important than ever in learning. The power of visual aids lies in the fact that they speak to another sense—the sense of sight. And the more senses you can involve in your presentation, the more memorable it will be.

"We talk too much; we should talk less and draw more."

—Johann Wolfgang von Goethe

An old axiom goes like this: "I hear and I forget. I see and I remember. I do and I learn." Apart from skill training sessions, many presentations don't lend themselves to the "doing" part of this learning sequence. Even so, nearly every presentation can be strengthened by the seeing, or visual, component. Visual aids allow your audience to absorb more information because you are speaking over more than one channel. They also have the advantage of helping your audience follow your outline and stay with you through transitions. They add variety and emphasis as well as interest. The old adage about a picture being worth a thousand words is true in many circumstances. The right visual aid can make your point concisely and attractively.

Types of Visual Aids

There are a variety of tools available to choose from when you're ready to incorporate a visual aid into your presentation. These range from low-tech and easily prepared to high-tech and elaborate. Here are some of your options:

- Flip charts
- An overhead projector
- Slides
- Videotapes and movies
- Computer-generated images
- Objects and models
- Posters, charts, and graphs

Each of these visual aids has strengths and weaknesses. Flip charts are an inexpensive and excellent way to record key ideas in meetings. They are also, unfortunately, bulky and awkward to travel with. The overhead projector is useful for groups of two hundred or more, depending on the room layout. It also has the advantage of projecting well with the lights on, avoiding the nap-inducing darkness that slides require. On the positive side, slides reproduce pictures well, can be used with large audiences to good effect, and can deliver a very smooth presentation. Increasingly sophisticated software mates the computer and overhead projector, allowing you to produce seamless visual aids, but such systems remain fairly expensive. Videotapes and movies can be very powerful—if well produced. The standards of most audiences for this kind of medium is quite high, and the cost of professional quality production is prohibitive for many presenters. Posters, charts, and graphs can be very effective ways to communicate quantifiable data, show trends, and highlight comparisons. There are a number of good software packages available that make these easy to prepare.

Factors that you need to weigh when considering which visual aid is appropriate for your presentation include the following:

- Audience size

- Room layout

- Expense

- Ease of use

- Portability

- Your comfort level with the medium

- The impact you want to make

Using Visual Aids

Once you settle on the medium you wish to use, keep in mind these simple ground rules, which apply to virtually any visual aid:

1. **Don't overdo it.** Well-prepared, professional looking visual aids can add a great deal to your presentation, but be wary of making them too complicated, and too busy. The guideline with visual aids is "less is more."

2. **Don't forget your audience.** The visual aids are there for your audience to look at, not for you to study. Maintain eye contact with your audience and keep your body turned toward the audience. Stand to one side if you need to point to a graph or other visual aid.

3. **Be aware of timing.** The goal is to have the strongest link possible between the aural and the visual. Turn on your projector (or flip the chart, etc.) just as you transition to the point your visual aid supports.

4. **Remember: That which can attract can also distract.** When you're finished making the point your visual aid supports, turn the projector off. Otherwise, it will distract your audience's attention from the new material you are presenting.

5. **Don't forget the star.** The visual aids are there to support and enhance the real star of the presentation—you! Don't overburden your presentation with visual aids that take away from the main event.

6. **Practice, practice, practice.** As with every other aspect of preparation, practice using your visual aids to improve your effectiveness.

Designing Visual Aids

How do you go about designing your visual aid? Here are some suggestions:

1. **Keep it lean and clean.** Use a separate visual aid for each point you want to make.

2. **Use white space generously.** A crowded visual leaves your audience (and you) searching for the important information. You want to highlight your point—not bury it.

3. **Use a balanced layout and design.** The same rules of good design that govern other publications apply to visual aids as well. Don't use too many typefaces or fonts. Create a focal point, and make it easy for the reader's eye to travel across the page, slide, or overhead.

You don't need to be a professional graphic designer to follow these basic principles. Many good books detailing basic design principles and approaches are available for the novice. Some of these are listed in the Bibliography of this book. The primary mistake many new presenters make is to overload their visual aids with text, competing images, or too much information. Lean and clean is the preferred mode.

Bob's sales managers left the kick-off meeting excited and enthused. They not only went away with a lot of necessary and important information, they also went away with a vivid, lasting picture in their minds. Such is the power of visual aids to add life, vitality, and energy to your presentation!

Apply It Now!

Add Visual Aids to Your Presentation

Think about the case study presentation you identified in Chapter 1. Either write out a brief answer to these questions or take the action suggested:

1. What kind of medium best suits your audience, subject, budget, and comfort level?

2. What "look" do you want your visual aid to have (e.g., humorous, classy, informal, colorful, etc.)?

_____

_____

3. Create a thumbnail sketch of how you'd like your visual aids to look.

4. Are you trying to tell a story with your visual aids? If so, how could you sequence your ideas and the visual aids that illustrate them?

_____

_____

_____

_____

_____

_____

5. Test your preliminary design against the rules of design noted in the text. What changes are called for?

_____

_____

_____

_____

6. Plan to have your visual aids produced in time to practice with them as you prepare. The visual aids need to be completed by:

_____

_____

Key Idea Chart

1. The most important ingredient in making a presentation interesting is that the presenter be interested in the material.

2. People love a good story.

3. A good illustration sheds light on your subject.

4. An analogy involves comparing two items from unrelated fields.

5. It's usually appropriate and often effective to include personal material or illustrations in a business presentation.

6. Nothing quite captures an audience's attention as effectively as judicious use of appropriate humor.

7. Pacing refers not only to your speed of delivery but also to the balance you strike between the emotional and factual component of your presentation.

8. Visual aids don't need to be high-tech to be effective. A simple flip chart or overhead can often help you drive your point home powerfully.

9. Write out below the key idea you got for yourself from Chapter 5.

_____

_____

_____

Chapter Six

Openings, Endings, and Transitions

Melissa is stuck and she's worried. Her presentation to the sales staff is only three days away, and things just aren't coming together. Early on, Melissa identified her theme and key points, and with some scrounging here and there and some creative brainstorming, she came up with some great stories and examples to illustrate her ideas. But she was stuck for a way to begin her presentation, and she was at a loss as to how to arrange the material in an orderly fashion that would progress to a clear and persuasive conclusion.

Those Crucial First Few Minutes— Your Opening

It's not fair, of course, that an audience forms its impression of you in the very first few minutes of your presentation. After all, you may have some pertinent information to deliver, some profound insights to share, or some persuasive arguments to make. But if you stumble coming out of the gate, you may lose the race. Consider for a moment your audience's agenda during the first five minutes of your presentation—all the unspoken questions they routinely bring to any presentation:

- Why should I listen to you?

- Is this going to be interesting?

- What are you talking about?

- Where are you headed?

- Do you have anything to say I need or want to hear?

- Do you know what you're talking about?

- Do you understand my needs and interests?

- Who are you?

- Are you genuine, credible, and sincere?

- How hard am I going to have to work to listen to you?

- So what?

This is not to suggest that most audiences are negative or critical. To the contrary, most audiences are sympathetic to a presenter, want the presenter to do well, and are eager to listen, learn, and laugh. But every audience approaches the speaker with some questions and with some degree of skepticism. It is your burden to address these concerns early on if you want to draw your listeners into your net.

"Speaking without thinking is shooting without aiming."

—W. G. Benham

You can lay to rest most of the above concerns if your opening does these three things:

- Grabs the attention and interest of the audience

- Establishes a common ground with the audience

- Notifies the audience of your theme and direction

Getting Your Audience's Attention

The first priority is to get your audience's attention and interest. The most effective openings reach out and figuratively grab the audience members by their lapels and either shout or whisper, "Pay attention!" Whether you have a history with your audience or they are strangers to you, the need to get their eyes, ears, and minds on what you're going to say is imperative. You can accomplish this in a number of different ways.

Here are some common attention-getting approaches speakers use to open their presentations:

- Anecdotes or stories

- Pertinent, interesting quotations or statistics

- Rhetorical questions

- Jokes or humor

- Questions designed to solicit verbal responses

Opening with an anecdote or story is a good way to get your audience's attention because nearly everyone loves a story. Anecdotes and stories are also a good way to notify your audience of your theme and direction. The more personal the story the better in most instances. Just be sure it relates directly to the main point you want to make.

As Melissa thought more about her presentation to the sales staff, she decided to open with a personal story. "About five years ago, I was trying to close what, for me, would have been the biggest contract I'd ever written. The client seemed convinced our company was right for its needs. I'd done my homework and made the best presentation to them I'd ever made. There was only one small detail we were still negotiating. Everything seemed to be moving ahead smoothly, until… " Her sales staff tuned in. She was talking out of her experience and that helped them believe she might have something of value to say.

Quotations and statistics can also be effective openers. If you open with a quote, be sure it is accurate and identify your source. If you're going to be presenting often, it's worth the time to start your own file of usable quotes on the topics you frequently address. One source of quotes that's often overlooked is song lyrics. Although they may be familiar to your audience, they have the advantage of being arresting when used out of context.

Jim opened his presentation to his maintenance managers in the following manner. "The challenge before us that I want to address today was once summed up well by George Jones and Emmylou Harris when they sang, 'Castles tall. Houses small. Left alone, they all fall down.' Well, we don't have a castle tall or a house small, but we have one heck of a production facility—and it's our job to make sure it doesn't all fall down!"

For statistics to be effective openers, they must relate to the immediate concern of your audience or be unusual enough to pique their interest. Be wary of overdoing it with statistics. After three or four numbers, statistics can quickly overwhelm most people.

Susan was giving a presentation on effective telephone techniques. She opened with this statistic: "Did you know that according to a study by AT&T, a planned business call takes an average of seven minutes, while an unplanned one takes eleven minutes? You say, 'So what? What's four minutes?' Four minutes is 42 percent savings in time. Multiply that by the thousands of phone calls you make in a year and you're looking at a significant difference in your phone effectiveness." When you use statistics, you may want to combine them, as Susan did in this example, with rhetorical questions that immediately invite your audience to relate the statistics to their concerns.

Sometimes a rhetorical question can stand by itself as an effective opener. If you were attending a presentation about the changing nature of the workplace, which of the following might hook your interest?

- "Let me ask you a question. What would you think if I told you that in ten years most of you will not have an office and will be independent contractors rather than full-time employees of your businesses?"

- "What do you think is the most significant trend for the coming decade that will affect your workplace? Would you be surprised to learn that according to many researchers it is… "

- "What would you do if you had to choose between secure employment in a dead-end, go-nowhere job and higher-risk, skill-based independent contracting? What might be the deciding factors for you in that choice?"

As these examples illustrate, rhetorical questions can be very effective when you have limited time because they allow you to jump right into your subject. One caution. Opening with rhetorical questions may later limit your audience's willingness to respond to questions you actually want answered.

As noted in the last chapter, humor is an especially powerful communication tool and a humorous opening is the first choice of many experienced presenters. If you choose to use a joke or humorous anecdote, be sure it relates directly to your subject. Telling an unrelated joke just to get a laugh still leaves you needing to introduce your topic and creates an awkward break in continuity. As with stories, humor that is personal is often more effective than a joke, especially one that has made the rounds many times.

Another effective way to open is to engage your audience in dialogue. Asking questions and soliciting responses from the audience immediately engages them and involves them in the presentation. This works best, of course, with smaller groups, but it can sometimes be effective with large audiences. If you do solicit questions or comments from a larger audience, be sure to repeat what's been shared so everyone can hear. This way of opening requires you to think well on your feet and exercise firm leadership. Opening up discussion to the group also opens up the possibilities of you losing control of the group or letting the responses lead you off in directions you didn't intend.

Apply It Now!

Hooking Their Interest

Think about the case study presentation you identified in Chapter 1. Brainstorm some ways you could hook your audience's interest in the subject. List key words or phrases for the following five possibilities.

1. An anecdote or story:

_____

_____

_____

_____

_____

_____

2. Quotation or statistic:

_____

_____

_____

_____

_____

_____

3. Rhetorical question:

_____

_____

_____

_____

_____

_____

4. Joke or humorous episode:

_____

_____

_____

_____

_____

_____

5. Question/response:

_____

_____

_____

_____

_____

_____

Establishing a Common Ground With Your Audience

Of course, if getting your audience's attention were the only goal of your opening, you could simply fire off a starter's pistol. You'd have their attention, to be sure! But you would also have sabotaged your second goal, which is to establish a common ground with your audience.

The challenge is to build a bridge to your listeners. If you are addressing people you work with every day and if you've made presentations to them previously, they will, hopefully, be disposed to tune in to you and hear what you have to say. But even with a familiar audience, it's good to deliberately try to build a bridge—a bridge from you and your subject to your audience and its needs. When you and your audience are unfamiliar with each other, this is even more imperative.

How do you establish common ground with your audience? How do you build a bridge across the gulf that naturally separates a presenter from his or her audience? That chasm is spanned by two planks:

- A shared interest

- A genuineness that affirms your credibility

You build rapport and interest with your audience when you let them know you share a common concern, interest, problem, passion, dilemma, activity, or pursuit. You want to make this clear in your opening by actually naming this concern. You are saying: "Listen to me because you and I share something in common. We have similar needs, aspirations, frustrations, or interests." Even in situations where you might be addressing a group with an interest or viewpoint that's different from your own, you can connect by clearly identifying *what* you share a stake in, however different your *perspectives*.

115

Exercise #10:

Identify Shared Interests

Think about the audience you will most likely address next or one you wish you could address. List below both the elements you have in common as well as those you share differences on. Consider how these areas of agreement and disagreement might influence your ability to find common ground with the audience.

	Similar	**Dissimilar**
Interests		
Problems		
Values		
Educational backgrounds		
Financial interests		
Motivations		
Race		
Gender		
Age		

If you were to address this group, which of the above similarities could serve as a point of contact, a common ground you could stand on, especially in your opening?

_____

_____

_____

_____

_____

_____

_____

_____

_____

_____

_____

_____

_____

_____

_____

_____

_____

_____

The other gateway to finding a common ground with your audience is to convey a genuineness of attitude that affirms your credibility. This does not mean devaluing or minimizing your expertise, professionalism, or specialized knowledge. After all, you wouldn't have been asked to make a presentation unless you had some information or insight to share that the group didn't already possess. Nor is this a call to a kind of faked familiarity or false humility, which audiences see through in a moment. Rather, it is an invitation to genuineness and authenticity. The greatest gift you have to give an audience, besides the information you want to impart, is the gift of yourself—your own unique style, perspective, personality, viewpoint, and energy.

This element is difficult to describe, but easy to spot. It's especially conspicuous by its absence. Perhaps you've sat through a presentation in which the presenter spoke the right words, but something seemed off nonetheless. The presenter may have been an "expert," but just didn't seem very credible or "real." Perhaps the speaker even came off as aloof and condescending. Or maybe you've had the opposite experience. Perhaps you've heard a genuine expert, an acknowledged authority. But in addition to expertise, the person's humanity was evident. His or her credibility wasn't just a matter of credentials.

All presenters can increase their capacity to convey a genuine attitude and thus increase their credibility—and their ability to connect with their audience. Two ingredients are particularly important. The first is to be real, to be authentically you. While you can learn much from observing others' styles of presenting, you must forge your own unique way of presenting yourself and your ideas to your audience. Being yourself is more important than being witty, being clever, or being technically polished. Don't be afraid to experiment with your own unique style of presenting. When you are uniquely you, you'll be at your best. Conversely, when you are at your best, you will be uniquely you.

Complete Exercise #11 to identify your personal characteristics that would make you seem most genuine to your audience.

"If you tell every step, you will make a long journey of it."

—Thomas Fuller

Exercise #11:

Being "Real" Self-Assessment

From the following list, circle the ten items you feel best describe you. (Copy the list before you circle anything, if you want your friends to do the exercise as well.)

Honest	Searching	Well-informed
Flexible	Caring	Cautious
Assertive	Persuasive	Direct
Serious	Forceful	Thoughtful
Optimistic	Sensitive	Friendly
Private	Bold	Realistic
Witty	Tactful	Centered
Enthusiastic	Reflective	Extroverted
Creative	Dependable	Sober-minded
Analytical		

Now put an "X" by four of the circled elements you think would most color your style of presenting and would most come across as "real" to an audience. Take a risk. Get two or three friends to circle the ones they think best describe you as well.

A second good way to establish a shared humanity with audience members is to relate to them on a personal level. As noted previously, being personal and being professional aren't mutually exclusive. Look for personal anecdotes and illustrations that could establish common ground between you and your audience. And don't be afraid to let your personal stake in your material be evident.

Another tool for conveying a genuine attitude that affirms your credibility is as close as your face. Remember that your nonverbal gestures and expressions communicate far more than the actual words you choose. A friendly smile, twinkling eyes, eye contact, and an open posture all say to the audience: "I'm here. I'm real. And I want to communicate with you."

Being authentically you, letting your own uniqueness shape and color your material, and letting it show on your face are among the most powerful ingredients for launching an effective opening. They can also weave a thread of integrity throughout your whole presentation. The more comfortable you are in front of your audience, the more comfortable they will be and, in turn, the more receptive they will be to your ideas and content.

Notifying the Audience of Your Theme and Direction

In addition to capturing your audience's attention and establishing a common bond with them, you'll also want to use your opening to notify the audience of your theme and direction.

Tell them what you're going to tell them. Tell them. And tell them what you told them. So goes an old axiom of speech organization. A good opening tells your audience what you're going to tell them. It alerts them to your primary concern, the focus or theme of your presentation, and the major points you intend to make. It's like a travel brochure. It paints an inviting picture of the destination and the highlights of the journey, without spoiling the surprises of the trip.

Usually, the best way to "tell" your audience is to use a rather straightforward approach that simply announces the theme and enumerates any major subpoints, as in the following examples:

"This morning we're going to look at the pros and cons of franchising our concept. I hope that by the time we're done, you'll agree with me that it's time to move ahead and risk franchising."

"There are three elements essential for an effective opening—getting the audiences' attention, finding a common ground, and identifying your direction. In other words, you want to grab them, hug them, and show them the map."

"Our concern this afternoon is with setting new sales quotas. We'll look first at last year's quotas, then we'll focus on the past three month's figures, and then we'll do some preliminary forecasting."

"I want you to go with me this evening on a journey to one of the hidden places of the human heart—to look together at four of the fears that most constrain our creativity and ingenuity."

"I'm going to give you the three "Ps" that make buying from us the smart choice. We'll look at Performance, Price, and People (our support staff)."

It takes but a moment to lay out your direction for your audience. In fact, it may take you no more than a sentence or two, as the examples show. But it's time you'll spend well, because it gives your audience a map. It not only alerts them to your overall theme and destination but also points out the main stops along the way, the subpoints you'll be making. A clear opening helps your audience see the big picture and how the various pieces of your presentation will fit together. It also helps them stay with you through transitions.

If you've written out your theme and purpose statements and identified your key points (see Chapters 3 and 4), you can readily summarize this information for use in your opening. Keep it simple. Just ask yourself this question: "What am I going to tell them?" Then write out your answer in no more than two sentences. Get some practice by completing the Apply It Now! exercise on the next page.

Apply It Now!

What Am I Going to Tell Them?

Think about the case study presentation you identified in Chapter 1. Look back over the theme and purpose statements you wrote in the exercises in Chapter 3 and the key points list you made in Chapter 4. Now, in one or two sentences, write what you want to tell your audience.

"I am going to tell them:

_____

_____

_____

_____

_____

_____

_____

_____

_____

_____

_____

_____

A good opening, then, gains the audience's attention, establishes a common ground with them, and alerts them to your theme. These three elements are not, of course, mutually exclusive—the most effective openings successfully blend these three elements. A well-told story, for example, can generate interest, establish rapport, and point to your overall theme. Some surprising statistics or an appropriate quotation can create curiosity, suggest your direction and, if offered with suitable levity or seriousness, convey warmth. Not every opening needs to have all three of these components in equal measure, but in general you will want to touch on these three elements in the first few minutes of your presentation.

Although many presenters don't write out their entire presentation, relying instead on an outline, you may find it helpful to write out your opening. Doing so will help you make it crisp, concise, and focused. Get started by completing the Apply It Now! exercise on the next page.

Apply It Now!
Write Your Opening

Think about the case study presentation you identified in Chapter 1. Look back over the exercises you have completed in this chapter. In the space below, write out a rough draft of your opening.

_____

_____

_____

_____

_____

_____

_____

_____

Now evaluate it by asking yourself these questions:

1. Will this grab the attention of the audience?

2. Have you built a bridge to them? Have you found a common ground with their concerns?

3. Have you notified them of your direction and theme?

Additional Opening Pointers

Begin your presentation with energy. Varying degrees of enthusiasm and sparkle are appropriate for different settings, topics, audiences, and presenter's personalities, but a warm smile, an erect and confident posture, animated body movement and gestures, eye contact with audience members, and genuine enthusiasm all help the audience connect with you.

If you begin with a soft, subdued voice, lackluster energy, and hesitation, you will be inviting your audience to tune out—so start out strongly and confidently. If you don't feel confident, follow the wisdom of many of the Twelve-Step programs—fake it till you make it! Being energetic and enthusiastic isn't the same as being phony or unauthentic. Rather, it is the strategy of deliberately acting your way into new feelings. It is consciously projecting energy to help you overcome your fears, misgivings, and any inner critical voices. Remember, if you don't believe in your own material and aren't excited about it, why should your audience be? Invite them to enter into your presentation by beginning with positive, visible energy.

Two cautions concerning your opening are worth keeping in mind. One is, don't apologize. Perhaps you haven't had the opportunity to prepare as thoroughly as you'd have liked. Maybe you're feeling hesitant or scared or uncertain. Maybe you were called on at the last minute to substitute for someone else. Generally, it's better not to mention any of these things. Instead, get on with the business of giving the best presentation you're capable of. Remember, your goal in the opening is to make contact with the audience, hook their interest, and let them know where you're going. Apologies generally don't help you reach any of these goals, so forego them. The exception to this might be when external factors have caused you to arrive late or when your audience is accommodating an uncomfortable setting or surroundings. A sincere, but brief apology in those circumstances might be in order, but then quickly move on to your presentation.

The second caution is this: don't prolong your opening. A strong, solid opening takes no more than a few minutes at most to present. A rambling, extended introduction to your presentation can erode audience interest and make your talk unnecessarily long. Sometimes you may need no more than a few sentences to connect with audience members, point them in the direction you'll be going, and then begin the journey. When it comes to the opening, quality—not quantity—is the measure that's important.

Endings

If the purpose of your opening is to "tell them what you're going to tell them," then the purpose of your ending is to "tell them what you told them." As you close your presentation, be sure to draw your key ideas together by reviewing and summarizing them.

In Chapter 3 you looked at writing a theme statement and a purpose statement. The theme statement, of course, summarizes what you want to communicate. The purpose statement defines the change you are seeking from your audience. For example, you may be asking your listeners to take a step, sign a contract, consider an option, agree to a plan, buy a product, take a risk, or make a commitment. If you begin with these ends in mind, you will have already done a great deal of the preparation required to successfully write the closing to your presentation. A good closing simply reiterates in a concise form your theme and purpose. It says, in effect, "Here's what I hope you'll remember, and here's what I hope you'll do." Sometimes your ending can be as simple and straightforward as that.

For example, a sales manager summarized her presentation by saying: "We began by examining the marketplace, and we saw that the indicators are very positive for our industry. We also looked at how terrific our new product line is. We beat the competition in quality and in pricing. We showed that our new training program is unparalleled in the industry."

This was her theme—the key ideas she wanted to communicate. But then she turned to her purpose, the change or action she wanted from her audience:

"In light of the growing market, the great products, and the first-rate training we'll be making available, we want each of you to set a challenging goal for yourself for this next quarter. Put it in writing and be specific. Then we'll meet one to one over the next few days to go over your goal and reach agreement on it. Stretch yourselves. Go for the gold. Don't settle for second best. Set a goal that will require your very best efforts. Then let's team together and go for it!"

When you're summarizing or recapping your main points, it's usually best to do so in the same order in which you presented the ideas, beginning at the start of your presentation and moving through successive points. Make this part of your closing very concise and clear.

There are at least a couple of ways to summarize your message. For instance, you can walk your listeners back through your key points. This is what the sales manager did in the previous example. Another summarizing technique is to simply enumerate your key idea, as in the following example:

"I have said there are three keys to our success. First, our performance. Second, our price. And finally, our people."

In the previous example, the presenter might have used alliteration to help memory retention:

"Remember the three 'Ps': Performance. Price. And our People!"

Not every presentation, of course, has two or three clearly distinct points. Sometimes a presentation centers on only one key idea, approached from a variety of angles or perspectives. In closing that kind of presentation, be sure to highlight that central idea one final time, very directly.

"My point, then, is that we must risk this step if we are to remain competitive!"

Or, "I'm sure it's clear by now how strongly I feel that we must risk this step..."

Or, "We've looked at the necessity of risking this step from several vantage points..."

Likewise, when it comes to the call to action part of your closing, be concise and specific. The most obvious instance of this need is the sales presentation. No close, no sale. At some point, you have to risk asking for a decision. But what some presenters overlook is that *every* presentation involves a close. If you're not asking your listeners to buy something, you're probably asking them to decide something—to decide for or against your idea, your proposal, or your recommendation. If you're not asking them to decide, you're probably asking them to change—to change a perception, a belief, an attitude, a pattern of action, an opinion. One of the keys to ending effectively is to be clear and specific about just what you're asking your audience to do.

Exercise #12:

Action-Focused Endings

1. In the following examples, what's the specific action or change the presenter is calling for? Circle the key verb or phrase.

   • "Take this information and apply it today. Take what I've shared with you and modify the planning process you're using with your clients. I think you'll be pleased with the results."

   • "We don't have to reach consensus on this today, but I want each of you to consider the options we've looked at. Which one do you think would best meet the company's needs? Think about it. Then on Thursday, let's get back together and make a decision."

   • "If this campaign is going to be successful, we're going to need some volunteers. There's a sign-up sheet out in the foyer. Before you leave here today, I hope you'll put your name down as someone we can count on for support in this crucial undertaking."

2. Now brainstorm ten verbs you could use to close a presentation that would invite or summon your listeners to change or act in some way.

_____

_____

_____

_____

_____

_____

_____

_____

_____

_____

_____

_____

_____

_____

_____

_____

_____

_____

_____

The most effective endings combine the summary statement with the call to action in a seamless closing. There are two typical patterns used:

Pattern A: "Here's what I told you, and here's what I want you to do."

Pattern B: "Here's what I want you to do, based on what I told you."

Another very effective way to combine your summary statement and call to action is to end with a story or anecdote that sums up your key ideas or indirectly challenges your listeners to action. People will remember your illustrations long after they have forgotten your carefully arranged, neatly ordered, logically interdependent subpoints. This is especially true when it comes to inspirational or motivational presentations, but it can also be true of other types of presentations. While direct appeals to action are usually preferable, sometimes a more "back-door" approach can be even more effective. Tell a story that illustrates the point you've been making or focuses the need for action. Then let the audience draw its own conclusions.

Stories appeal to the heart as well as the head, and they offer your listeners concrete images rather than amorphous ideas. If you are, indeed, presenting with the hope of affecting change in your audience, then it is appropriate to think in terms of inspiration as well as information, to aim at touching the emotions as well as the intellect. Painting word pictures, sharing a personal anecdote, using a picture or illustration on the overhead, narrating a story, or closing with a humorous incident or joke can all be powerful ways to end your presentation.

Another effective tool for ending your presentation is the wrap-around. When you use a wrap-around, you pick back up on a story, image, metaphor, or illustration you used earlier to open your presentation or make a key point. One benefit of using a wrap-around is that you get double mileage from the image. It serves both to introduce an idea and to fix the idea in your audience's mind. The wrap-around brackets, as it were, your whole presentation, creating a unity between the beginning and the end.

John introduced his presentation on the need for life-long education by talking about his father's skills as a handyman and his remarkable tool collection. At the end of his presentation, he used a wrap-around, returning to the image of his father's tools.

"Security today isn't found in where you work or who you work for," he said. "Rather it's found in having a well-balanced collection of tools, constantly sharpening them, and using them diligently. Just like my father taught me, you can't fix everything with a hammer. I hope you will decide today to keep adding to your tool collection—for your sake and for the sake of the work that must be done for our company and nation to go forward."

"Charm + wit + levity may help you at the start; but at the end, it's brevity that wins the public's heart."

—R. Cheney

One final word about endings. When you've said what you came to say, stop. Many fine and well-constructed presentations have been rendered ineffectual because the presenter rambled on and let the presentation dribble out, rather than drawing it to a crisp, clear, and definite conclusion. An old axiom of presentation skills goes like this: "To be seen, stand up. To be heard, speak up. To be appreciated, shut up!" Again, when you have said what you came to say, stop. Tell them what you told them in a brief summary statement that underscores your key points and focuses on the change or action you're calling for. Or use a good concluding story or illustration. And then simply stop.

Use the Apply It Now! exercise on the next page to write an ending for one of your presentations.

"Get up, speak up, shut up, and sit down."
—Toastmasters International

Apply It Now!
Write Your Ending

Think about the case study presentation you identified in Chapter 1. Look back over the theme statement and purpose statement exercises you completed in Chapter 2. Then write out a rough draft of your ending.

_____

_____

_____

_____

_____

Now, evaluate your ending by asking yourself these questions:

1. Have you summed up or recapped your main point or points?

2. What change or action are you asking your audience to undertake?

3. How concrete and specific is the change you've called for? How could you make it more specific?

4. Have you used a story or illustration? If not, can you think of one that would tie your presentation together?

5. Have you appealed to the emotions as well as the intellect in your ending?

Fine-Tune Your Transitions

If the purpose of your opening is to tell your listeners where you're going and the purpose of your ending is to remind them of where they've been (and, in the call to action part of your closing, to point to the next step), the purpose of transitions is to keep your audience oriented along the journey. Like road signs or a good map, effective transitions help your listeners navigate your presentation and keep their bearings. They serve to indicate changes in topic, direction, or emphasis.

As you've seen, most presentations involve one central idea that is developed or supported by a few subpoints. Transitions alert your audience as you move from one of these points to the next. They help your audience follow the flow of your ideas. Conversely, presentations without clear transitions seem to run together in a confusing jumble of words and ideas like a sentence without spaces or punctuation.

But transitions have a value to the presenter as well as to the audience. Thinking carefully through your transitions imposes a discipline and structure that is invaluable in arranging your thoughts and organizing your presentation. By identifying the main components of your presentation and the points at which you will need to transition, you'll save your talk from becoming a rambling monologue. If you're not clear about your transitions, then you can be sure your audience will likewise be confused and have a hard time tracking with you.

Transitions occur naturally between:

- Your opening and the body of your presentation.
- The main points of your talk.
- Ideas and illustrations.
- The body and ending.

Have you ever driven a car equipped with a manual transmission? You can tell when it's time to shift because either the tachometer or the sound of the engine alerts you. But the goal is to get on to the next gear, not to spend much time shifting. If you shift too abruptly, of course, you may grind the gears and things may get a bit jerky. On the other hand, if you shift too slowly, you may lose momentum. So you want to shift at just the right time. You also want to shift smoothly. And you don't want to call a lot of attention to the actual shifting process—the focus really ought to be on the power and speed and progress of the car, not on the gears.

Making good transitions is a lot like that. You want to transition from one part of your presentation to the next at just the right time, and you want to do so smoothly. But not so smoothly that no one realizes you shifted gears. And you don't want to call attention to the transition itself. Its only purpose is to get your presentation further down the road.

How do you transition smoothly from one part of your presentation to the next? Mainly, you rely on verbal cues—phrases that alert your audience to a change of course or direction. Here are some examples:

- "First, let's look at…"
- "First off, I want to mention…"

- "Second, you should consider…"
- "A final issue we need to look at is…"
- "Next, direct your attention to…"
- "Now if we have X, it then follows that…"
- "My first (second, third, etc.) point is…"
- "Finally, we need to be aware of…"
- "Having looked at X, now let's turn our attention to…"
- "Before we move on to Y, are there any questions about X?"
- "If X is true, then it seems logical that…"
- "In addition to X, there is Y…"

In addition to these verbal signals, be aware of the power of the nonverbal. A shift in your body posture can alert your audience to a shift of focus. Likewise, a change in tone of voice or inflection can telegraph your intent. Pauses can also effectively mark transitions. When enumerating several points, some speakers will count the points off on their fingers as they review them. If you are using any audiovisual aids, such as an outline on an overhead, you can signal transitions by gradually uncovering each segment of the presentation as you go along.

Acronyms, alliteration, and rhyming words can also help mark your transitions. Here's an example of how to transition using an acronym:

"That covers the 'I' of ACTION goals. Now let's look at the 'O' and 'N'—ownership and negotiated."

Alliteration can also allow smooth transitions:

"So far we've looked at the price of preparation. Now let's consider the payoff of preparation..."

An example of transitioning via rhyming is this: "We've looked at the effects of burnout—how workers expire. Now let's look at "rust out" and how workers tire."

The transition between your opening and the body of your presentation can often be a very smooth and natural one. Perhaps you began with a story or a straightforward account of your material. You then simply transition with a brief phrase such as, "Let's look first at... "

Transitioning from a point to an illustration of that point often takes no more than a simple phrase such as, "For example..." or "The following story makes the point clear... " If you've aptly chosen your illustration, it may require no transitional phrase at all. Simply begin the story or illustration. Its tie to the previous material will be self-evident to your audience.

Transitioning from the body of your presentation to the closing can be accomplished with phrases similar to these:

- "In conclusion, then..."
- "In summary..."
- "I've pointed out two key elements..."
- "Finally..."
- "By way of review..."
- "What we've seen is that..."

Apply It Now!

Where Will You Need Transitions?

Think about the case study presentation you identified in Chapter 1. Look back over the Organize and Outline exercise you completed in Chapter 4. Indicate on that outline the places where you will need clear transitions. Write out below some key phrases or words you could use.

1. Between your opening and first point:

   _____

   _____

   _____

2. Between your main points:

   _____

   _____

   _____

3. Between the body of your talk and your closing:

   _____

   _____

   _____

Key Idea Chart

1. The first priority of your opening is to get the audience's attention.

2. Early on, identify for your audience your shared interest or concern.

3. One of the most powerful ways to connect with your audience is to simply be authentic.

4. A good opening tells your audience what you're going to tell them.

5. In addition to summarizing your presentation, a good ending makes clear to your listener's what you are asking them to do.

6. Transitions should guide your audience from one point or idea to the next in a presentation.

7. Write out below the key idea you got for yourself from Chapter 6.

_____

_____

_____

_____

_____

_____

_____

Chapter Seven

Preparing for the Unpredictable

J im is nearly finished with his presentation. He has presented what he believes to be five compelling reasons the board of directors should hire a full-time executive director. Just as he's about to transition to his conclusion and wrap up his presentation, John, the board member with the longest reign, raises his hand, and without being recognized, asks rather loudly, "And what makes you think hiring someone is going to solve all our problems? Seems to me it could just make our problems worse. We're a not-for-profit organization, but that doesn't mean we don't have to watch the bottom line, you know. Just where do you think that additional money is going to come from anyway?"

Jim feels the flush of anger wash over him. "Why does John always have to be so negative?" he asks himself. "Hasn't he been listening? I've already explained where the money would come from."

But before Jim can respond, John steps in again. "And besides, young man, we've gotten along just fine until now without a full-time staff member. No reason to do something different now. If it isn't broken, don't fix it, I always say."

This is what Jim would like to say: "I'll tell you what's broken. You are. You are a broken record. Every meeting it's the same old stuff. Why we can't do this. Why we can't do that. Why this won't work. Why that won't work. John, I'm sick of your negativity and I'm sick of you!"

This is what Jim realizes: "Alienating John would be the very last thing I could afford to do if I want to sell my proposal. If I told John what I thought, I'd make a fool of myself before the entire board of directors."

Jim suddenly realizes that he hasn't adequately prepared himself to answer questions and objections. "Why didn't I anticipate John and his negativity ahead of time?" he wonders to himself.

Not every audience includes a John. But nearly every audience includes some people who may have some questions about your presentation or some objections to the ideas you're selling. Being prepared to handle these can mean the difference between a successful presentation and a nightmare.

Understand, first of all, the difference between a question and an objection. A question is a request for additional information or clarification. An objection is a stated challenge or disagreement with something you've said. Not all questions, of course, are questions. Sometimes they are statements or objections simply disguised as questions. But whether it's a straightforward question, a disguised objection, or a straightforward objection, the key to successfully handling it is to be prepared.

Handling Questions and Objections

Here are fourteen tips for handling questions and objections:

1. ***Welcome questions and objections.*** Questions and objections, properly prepared for, need not be feared. To the contrary, you can welcome them because they:

   - Give you an opportunity to demonstrate your confidence and competence.

   - Afford you an opportunity to further persuade your audience and win over some reluctant minds.

   - Identify areas needing clarification.

   - Are evidence that your audience is interested. Salespeople, in fact, see objections as a very positive sign that the customer is interested. If he or she weren't interested to some degree, there would be no reason to object!

   - Provide an opportunity to turn a monologue into a dialogue to everyone's profit.

2. ***Anticipate questions and objections.*** Certain kinds of presentations are usually protected from questions and objections—keynote addresses, for example. But even if you're certain you won't face any questions, it's still a good idea to anticipate them. Why? Because you might be surprised. A question might be asked even though it isn't appropriate. Even in situations protected from public questions, you may be asked questions privately after your presentation or during a break.

"If anything can go wrong, it will."

—Murphy's Law

An even more important reason for anticipating questions and objections is to strengthen your presentation. If you've carefully thought through the kinds of questions and objections your audience may have and formulated appropriate responses, you can incorporate much of this material into your presentation, strengthening it and making it more persuasive.

Put yourself in your listener's place. Ask yourself these kinds of questions:

- What concerns will they have?

- Who will most likely disagree with my proposal? Why?

- If I hadn't already researched this so much, what questions would I have?

- What technical material or jargon is likely to be unclear or confusing?

- If I were on the other side of the table, what would my objections be?

You won't be able to anticipate every objection and question, but if you have prepared well, you'll be ready for most of them.

3. ***Listen to questions and objections.*** Pay attention! When confronted with a question or objection, your first tendency will be to start thinking about your answer. Don't! Your first obligation is to fully hear the question. Let the person finish. An obvious exception to this would be a situation in which a person, under the guise of a question, begins to give a personal speech. In that circumstance, you would want to interrupt and regain control.

4. *Restate questions and objections.* This has at least three
values. First, it lets the person know he or she has been
heard and taken seriously. With some objections, that is
about 90 percent of what the person needs—simply to be
heard more than given an "answer." Second, repeating the
question ensures that others in the audience have had an
opportunity to hear it. Finally, restating a question or
objection buys you time to formulate your response.

One way to restate a question is to repeat a person's own
words. You can seldom go wrong with this verbatim
approach because it's the response style that says most
clearly to the person that you were really listening. Also,
this approach is best if you're fielding a hostile or negative
question or objection. A person who is upset needs to hear
his or her own words repeated with a minimum of
interpretation.

A second approach is to recap the questioner's words. In
this case, you put what was said into your own words,
summarizing the essence of the communication. This is
especially useful if the questioner has been wordy or repetitive.

A third approach is to listen actively. In active listening, you
respond less to the verbal content and more to the feeling
or emotional content of the question or objection. If a
questioner has asked multiple questions, it's okay to pare
them down to just one question and indicate that you could
perhaps respond to the others after the meeting.

Exercise #13 on the next page will help you distinguish among
the three approaches.

Exercise #13:

Listening Responses to Questions and Objections

Read the following question and the responses that follow. Beside each response, indicate whether you think it's a verbatim response (V), a recap response (R), or an active listening (AL) response.

Questioner:

"You said that good communication is essential to working together as a team. But what do you do when you work for a boss who simply won't listen to you? He is very opinionated and controlling. He's forever giving orders, but when I bring a concern or problem to him, I might as well be talking to a wall. What do you do in a situation like that?"

Responses:

____ 1. "What I hear you saying is that it's really frustrating to try to communicate with someone who's all mouth and no ears! It feels futile to even try."

____ 2. "Your boss won't listen to you. He has lots of opinions and gives lots of orders, but talking to him is like talking to a wall."

____ 3. "Your question is what to do when you have a boss who either can't or won't listen to you and your ideas."

5. *Gather your thoughts before you respond to questions and objections.* Follow this order:

- Listen.

- Repeat the question or objection.

- Pause and think.

- Respond.

If you're formulating your response while the questioner is talking, you may miss important information. So listen well and repeat the question back. Then give yourself a moment to think. It may be helpful to breathe deeply and simply pause momentarily. Let your thoughts come. Take a sip of water if you need more time. Use a simple lead in such as, "That's an interesting point you raise," or "That's a question I frequently get asked," or "I'm glad you asked that…" The key is to respond, not react. Pausing for even a brief moment can help, especially if the objection or question had a negative edge to it.

6. *Respond directly to questions and objections.* Look at the questioner, initially, but also include the rest of the audience in your eye contact so it doesn't become a two-person conversation. (In fact, it's usually better not to end your response while still looking at the questioner. That sometimes elicits yet another question.) Then respond directly to the question or objection. Be brief and to the point and give your best answer. Use your best people and diplomacy skills.

"Be prepared."
—Motto of the Boy Scouts of America

7. ***If you don't know the answer to a question or objection, say so.*** It's better to give an honest "I don't know" response than it is to try and bluff your way through. Here are some other options if you don't know an answer:

- Elicit responses from others in the audience. ("That's a tough one. Does anyone here have some good ideas on this?")

- Suggest that you talk during the break or after the meeting. ("I'll need to give that one some thought. Why don't you catch me afterwards and we'll talk about that?")

- Say you'll have to get back with an answer. ("I'll need to do some more homework on that one. Afterwards, if you'd like to give me your name and address, I'll get back to you.")

- List the question on the overhead or flip chart and say you'll come back to the question if there's time. ("That's one I don't have a good answer for right now. I'll list it here, and if there's time, we'll come back to it at the end.")

8. ***Stay in control of questions and objections.*** You don't want to turn over your presentation to someone with a lot of questions or to a vocal objector. How long you should wait before responding to a question or objection depends a great deal on the circumstances. If you're making a sales presentation to a client, you might want to answer objections indefinitely. But if it's a public presentation and a person's question seems out of the mainstream of your audience's interest, you'd want to keep the question and answer very brief. While there's room for exceptions, a good guideline is to allow no more than two exchanges. The audience member asks a question or makes a brief comment. You respond. The audience member responds. You respond. And then move on. In many situations, to go beyond that is to risk entering into a two-way conversation that loses the interest of the rest of the audience.

An alert, assertive posture, direct eye contact, and a confident tone of voice can help keep you in control. Also, don't be afraid to interrupt if the person is being repetitive, going on at great length, or launching into his or her own presentation. After all, it's your presentation, not theirs. Several phrases can be useful when you need to interrupt a questioner. You might experiment with some of these:

- "Excuse me."

- "Yes, yes."

- "Just a moment, please."

- "Wait!" (accompanied by an appropriate hand gesture)

- "Before you go further…"

- "Let me respond to that."

Once you get the person to stop talking, respond concisely, shift eye contact to someone else, and move on.

9. *Learn from questions and objections.* Other than formal, written evaluations, questions and objections are one of your best feedback mechanisms. Pay attention to them, especially commonly asked questions, and fine-tune your next presentation on that topic accordingly. Nine times out of ten, people raise an objection or ask a question out of genuine interest or concern, not malice. So be open to questions and let them guide how you fashion future presentations. One reason to welcome objections and

questions is the opportunity they give you to sharpen your content, your presentation skills, and your ability to think well on your feet.

10. ***Don't lose your temper or belittle the questioner.*** No matter how irrelevant, mean-spirited (remember, this is rare!), or just plain dumb the question or objection is, you hardly ever serve your purpose by belittling the questioner. The temptation to respond with a clever put-down, sarcasm, or outrage can, on occasion, be nearly overwhelming and can seem immensely gratifying. In the long run, however, doing so will diminish your credibility with your audience. For the most part, treat the questions and objections raised as if they are sincere and serious, even if it seems to you they are not. If it's patently obvious that the objector is trying to make a fool of you, don't respond in like manner. Interrupt if necessary, regain control of the situation, and move on. Your commitment to maintaining grace under fire will be noticed and admired by the other participants. Remember, too, that you are under no obligation to respond to every question or objection. It's always okay to say: "I'll pass on that one. Does anyone else have a question or comment?"

11. ***Don't say, "I've already covered that."*** While that may be true, to say to someone that you've already covered certain material is to imply that he or she wasn't listening well or isn't very smart. Instead, go ahead and give a very brief response and move on.

12. ***Don't drop the bomb on Luxembourg! Avoid overkill.*** Short, concise responses are the order of the day. When asked a well-framed question that pertains to the area of your expertise, the temptation is to give a lot of information.

Resist that temptation for the sake of the rest of your audience, who may not be as interested in as much detail as your questioner may be. You will seldom err if you aim for conciseness and brevity in your responses.

13. Don't compliment one questioner and not others.
"Thank you, that's a really good question" may seem like a natural response—and it often is. But if your next questioners don't hear those words of appreciation, they may feel they've asked a dumb question. Better to thank everyone or no one than to selectively praise some questioners.

14. Don't let yourself get trapped by either/or questions.
Sometimes an objector will try to pin you down by asking an either/or, yes/no kind of question. If one of those alternatives best describes your response, fine. But if not, always reserve the right to respond with a different option or opinion. Politicians are masters at this, often taking a reporter's very pointed either/or question and using it as a jumping off point to make whatever point the politician has in mind. Remember, you get to make whatever response you choose—it's your presentation.

Tips for Dealing With Objections

As noted, objections differ from questions in that they state a challenge or disagree with something you've said. Consider these ten additional ideas for responding to objections.

1. Understand why some people have objections. People may object to your ideas or proposal for a wide variety of reasons, often because they are looking at the same reality you have addressed, but from a very different point of view. If your information is new or unexpected to them, they need time to assimilate your data and perspective. They may not have the whole picture. They may find your ideas threatening. They may have a need to argue and control. They may be trying to impress others in the audience. They may have gotten up on the wrong side of the bed and their objection really has nothing to do with your presentation!

The point is not necessarily to play junior psychologist and decipher hidden and inner motives. But it will help you to respond to objections if you ask yourself: "What's going on here? What's really at stake? What might the real issue be?" Recognizing that people raise objections for a wide variety of reasons and with many different motives will help keep you flexible in your responses.

A second benefit of being aware of the many different reasons people raise objections is that it will help you take them less personally. It's easy to take any objection to your proposal or ideas as a personal rejection, but that's usually not the case. Even if the objector should question your motive or character, responding to the issues and content of the objection and not the personal dimension is usually best.

2. *Be prepared to deal with anger.* Sometimes an objector will be angry. If not evident in their words, it will be evident in their tone of voice or body language. You can defuse some of the anger by trying first to understand their concern. The most important thing you can do initially when someone objects angrily is to listen carefully and then let them know you have heard them.

You will also want to stay detached. As mentioned, separate the issue from yourself. Respond with empathy. "I hear that you are angry and don't like what I have proposed. I hear you saying that the cutbacks would be too severe and that your department simply couldn't fulfill its responsibilities with that kind of budget. I understand you are very upset."

3. *Zero in on the heart of the objection.* It's important to separate the wheat from the chaff. What is the core issue the objector is concerned about? You can get at this in a couple of ways. Ask for more information: "Say more about that, please," or "Let me hear more from you about that." This not only gives you more information, it also buys time for you to formulate your response. Another approach is to ask a closed-ended question. This can help narrow the focus. "Do you object to the proposed cutbacks themselves or the timetable for implementation?"

4. *Clarify the benefits of your proposal or further explain your ideas.* Once you have fully heard and understood the objection, give your best answer. Frame your response in terms of the positive benefits your proposal offers. Counter the concerns raised with an alternative interpretation, viewpoint, or perspective. Keep coming back to the main thrust of your presentation or proposal.

5. *Be aware of the words "but" and "and."* The word "but" negates what has come before it. "I hear you are concerned about the timetable for the budget cuts, but..." Often it's better to use "and." "I hear you are concerned about the timetable for the budget cuts. That's certainly a legitimate concern. And another factor to consider is what it may cost us to delay implementation. I wonder if there's a way to lessen the downside you've identified and still move forward in a timely manner?"

6. *If you're wrong, admit it.* If your objector is right and you have some facts wrong or your interpretation of them is incorrect, simply acknowledge it and move on.

7. *Look for a point of agreement.* This is a useful tool, sometimes called "bridging." You find a point of agreement or shared concern, articulate that point, and then bridge into points of disagreement. Sometimes this approach can move you and the objector into a mutual problem-solving mode rather than an adversarial mode.

8. *Respond indirectly.* Sometimes an objection is best dealt with by way of a story or analogy rather than with a direct response. A story or analogy can defuse the personal dimension of some objections and invites the listener to consider the matter from another perspective altogether.

9. *Don't get stuck.* Once you've offered your best response to an objection, move on. End eye contact and move on to the next person, or end the question and comment time. It's okay to ignore a raised hand and say simply: "That's all the time we're going to take for questions and comments now. If you'd like to talk more, I'll be available after the meeting is over."

10. *Name the nastiness.* As noted, most objectors aren't mean-spirited. But sometimes you will run across someone who is. If you encounter a very vocal and provocative antagonist, it's usually better not to respond in kind. Don't get hooked by these kinds of objections. Instead, stay on topic, and deal with the substantive issues. On some occasions, however, you may need to call the person's bluff, especially if the person is taking potshots at you or engaging in side conversations or sarcasm. A straightforward, direct

confrontation is usually best. One way to do this is to simply name out loud what you are experiencing and see going on, as in these examples:

"Bob, I hear you saying that not only do you think my plan stinks, you think I'm incompetent for having proposed it. Is that what you're saying?"

"Sir, it seems you have a lot of responses to what I'm saying. Would you share those with the whole group and not just the person next to you? Your side conversation is distracting."

"Jim, I understand you don't like my ideas. What I want is for you to confine your comments to the content of my proposal and not your assessment of my intelligence. I'm willing to debate the issues; I'm not willing to be insulted."

"Ma'am, I'm going to have to ask you to stop. Our time is up and we can't really deal with those concerns at this moment. If you want to write to me, I'll consider your suggestions."

The key idea is to maintain your dignity and to assert yourself strongly and directly enough to maintain control of the situation.

Complete the Apply It Now! exercise on the next page to prepare for questions and objections you might encounter in your case study presentation.

Apply It Now!

Prepare for Questions and Objections

Think about the case study presentation you identified in Chapter 1. List below three questions or objections that you think your audience might likely raise.

1. _____
   _____
   _____
   _____

2. _____
   _____
   _____
   _____
   _____

3. _____
   _____
   _____
   _____

What would your response be? Write out your response to each one and then decide if you want to incorporate it into the body of your presentation. If not, go over your responses so you will be prepared if these questions or objections are raised.

_____

_____

_____

_____

_____

_____

_____

_____

_____

_____

_____

_____

_____

_____

Surprise! Surprise!

In addition to questions and objections, occasionally you may have to deal with other unexpected and unplanned interruptions to your presentation. These fall into three broad categories: technical problems, people problems, and weird happenings.

Most technical problems can be prevented by adequate preparation. Check all of your audiovisual equipment ahead of time and plan for contingencies such as a burned out overhead projector bulb. Also check the lighting, temperature, and room accommodations for your audience. If you're meeting in a public facility, know whom to contact should problems arise, such as if you need to adjust the room temperature. A Facilities Checklist is included in Appendix C.

Even when you've prepared well, problems can sometimes arise. A microphone may suddenly go dead, outside radio signals may come in over the sound system, a sudden power failure may leave you in darkness—these and stranger things have happened. Handle such situations with as much grace and good humor as you can, trusting that your audience will be impressed if you demonstrate flexibility, ingenuity in problem solving, and the ability to laugh at absurd happenings. It's normal to experience some anxiety and confusion when the impossible happens, but insofar as possible, roll with the punches and look for the humor in the situation.

People problems can include not only unexpected questions and objections but also those rare instances in which someone wanders into your meeting place inadvertently, an audience member falls asleep and snores loudly, medical emergencies occur in the audience, you or someone in the audience is seized by a sneezing or coughing fit, children are present and become restless and disruptive, someone is intoxicated or high on drugs, and other unpredictable interruptions. Again, the goal is to handle the interruption with grace, dignity, and good humor. It's far better to stop your presentation and deal with the situation than try to forge ahead in the midst of a situation that is obviously distracting everyone. Depending on the circumstances, you might want to call upon an associate or friend to intervene. You might want to stop and address the problem directly. One alternative is to call a ten-minute break, deal with the problem person, and then reconvene. If necessary, call building security or the police. It's time to act when it's clear the interruption is distracting to your audience, that it's going to be more than momentary, and that no one else is taking steps to remedy the situation.

Situations involving noisy children are especially vexing. While they don't occur in business settings, they are surprisingly frequent in public presentations. There's always the hope the child will get quiet and the disruption will pass. But the longer it goes on and the louder it becomes, the harder it is to ignore for both you and your audience. On the other hand, there is always a reluctance to offend a parent by addressing the problem directly. More than one presenter has desperately wished a parent would remove an offending child, only to see them continue to sit there, seemingly oblivious to the problem being created, or worse yet, seeming to find their tyke's behavior amusing. If the situation goes on for more than a couple of minutes, it's often best to stop and directly and gently address the problem. "I'm sorry, but I'm afraid I need to ask you to take your child out. It seems he is not enjoying my presentation as much as I wished. I think he might be much happier if he didn't have to endure me any longer!" Said with a smile and a gentle tone of voice, you have done what you can. The parent may be offended, but better for one person to be offended than to have your whole presentation rendered ineffective.

Weird happenings include all other interruptions not already discussed. Some examples would be emergency vehicles parking outside with sirens blazing; pieces of ceiling tile falling; noise from a meeting next door; a late-breaking, important news announcement passing from person to person; and any number of other situations that are unpreventable. Presenters have been known to spill drinks, push over the podium or overhead projector, slip and fall, discover an unzipped zipper or other clothing in disarray, become ill, faint, mispronounce or accidentally twist words, stumble into double entendres, set their clothing afire with a candle, or otherwise create bedlam and great hilarity. The watchwords again are these: grace, dignity, and good humor. If you stumble and fall, figuratively or literally, pick yourself up, dust yourself off, enjoy a good laugh, and get on with your presentation.

Create your own worst-case scenario in Exercise #14 and then devise a plan for dealing with it professionally.

Exercise #14:

Dealing With the Unexpected

Let your imagination play. Picture yourself making a presentation when some calamity happens. Create your own "worst-case scenario." Write it below. Picture the scene unfolding. How would you respond? How could you draw out the humor in the situation? How would you assertively respond, if necessary? What would you say? What would you do? Rehearse this scene in your mind, reinforcing your inner picture of grace, dignity, and good humor.

Key Idea Chart

1. Questions and objections can actually help you strengthen the content of your presentation.

2. Objections often indicate interest and involvement.

3. Questions and objections are best handled when the presenter has taken time to anticipate them and prepare a response.

4. When dealing with questions and objections, it's important for the presenter to maintain control of the situation.

5. A presenter's first response to any question or objection is to be sure to listen well.

6. Three watchwords in dealing with unexpected technical problems, people interruptions, or weird happenings are grace, dignity, and humor.

7. Write out below the key idea you got for yourself from Chapter 7.

_____

_____

_____

_____

_____

_____

_____

Chapter Eight

Assembling the Pieces

Congratulations! You're in the home stretch. You've thought, researched, gathered sources, focused your theme and purpose, distilled your key points, gathered illustrations. You've thought through your opening, closing, and key transitions. You've anticipated questions, possible objections, and contingencies. Now it's time to put all the pieces together.

There are two main ways in which presenters draw it all together—an outline and a manuscript. There are advantages and disadvantages to both approaches, and the final decision hinges on what works best for you. If you're new to presenting, you may want to experiment with both approaches a few times to see what best fits your style. Whichever approach you choose, the goal is the same: to create a unified, coherent whole out of the raw stuff of your preparation.

Using an Outline

Many presenters do the final organizing of their material by outlining. In fact, if you've completed all the "Apply It Now!" exercises, you've already done a great deal of the work in completing your outline. An outline is like a skeleton. It's the bones, the supporting structure of your presentation. Your key points and illustrations are the meat on the bones. But it's the outline that allows your presentation to function as more than a hodgepodge collection of disparate parts, that allows it to cohere and become whole.

Many presenters prefer to speak from an outline rather than a manuscript, noting the greater freedom and flexibility it offers. An outline provides more opportunity for eye contact and isn't nearly as cumbersome to handle as a manuscript. Also, it generally doesn't take as long to prepare.

Keep the following six steps in mind as you prepare your outline:

1. The purpose of an outline is to guide you through your presentation. It can be pretty bare bones if you only have a few key ideas to remember and are well-acquainted with your material. Sometimes you need only to jot down a few key words to jog your memory should you need them. On the other hand, a more detailed outline works better for many other occasions. If you're presenting quite a bit of detailed information or covering a number of different points, a more comprehensive outline will probably serve you better. Outline your presentation in as much detail as you feel necessary in order to be in charge of your material and the flow of ideas, key points, and illustrations, from beginning to end.

2. Begin with the main body of your presentation. List out the key points you have decided to make. Identify each one by a key word or phrase. Remember to think in terms of your theme statement (which says *what* you want to communicate) and the purpose statement (which identifies the *change* you want from your audience). Make sure each of your points supports these two statements.

3. Next, add the stories, illustrations, data, or audiovisuals you will use to support those key points. Again, use key words or phrases to identify this supporting material. You might, for example, put in your outline: "Overhead: Last quarter's earning statement," or "Tell story of own experience in plant closing last fall."

4. Add your opening and closing. Since these are particularly crucial parts of your presentation, you may want to outline them in more detail or even consider writing them out.

5. Examine your transition points. Add any key words or phrases you may need to remember that will help you make smooth and clear transitions.

6. Prepare any tables, lists, or technical information. Indicate on your outline where these respective pieces of information will be used in the presentation.

"Whoever wants to see a brick must look at its pores, and must keep his eyes close to it. But whoever wants to see a cathedral cannot see it as he sees a brick. This demands respect for distance."

—José Ortega y Gasset

Apply It Now!

Outline Your Presentation

Think about the case study presentation you identified in Chapter 1. Refer back to the work you did in Chapter 4 in sequencing your main points. Now, outline your entire presentation. To aid you in doing so, the following sample outline is offered. Adapt it freely according to the number of key points you plan to make.

Opening

Transition to First Point

First Key Point

Illustrations or supporting materials

Transition to Second Point

Second Key Point

Illustrations or supporting materials

Transition to Third Point

Third Key Point

Illustrations or supporting materials

Transition to Closing

Closing

After you have completed a rough draft of your outline, evaluate it and fine-tune it by answering these questions:

1. Does my opening get people's attention and tell them where I'm going?

2. Do each of my key points support my theme and purpose statements?

3. Have I illustrated each key point in a way that it covers everything it should?

4. Have I concluded with a clear summary? Did I tell them what I told them?

5. Have I made clear the action or change I am asking for?

6. Are my transitions clear?

Writing a Manuscript

Some presenters prefer to write out their presentation in full, whether in long-hand or on a word processor. Writing out your presentation is one of the best ways to create a unified whole out of your constituent parts. It allows you to more carefully select words, which may be an important consideration in keynote or sensitive presentations requiring precision of phrasing. Manuscripts can be especially helpful in making transition points clear and smooth. Writing one out is a great discipline, forcing you to think through your entire talk from beginning to end. It also instills confidence. The thing is "nailed down." You know where you're going and what you're going to say. It also affords a sense of completion and closure.

On the downside, actually using a manuscript at the time of your presentation presents some challenges. You don't want to simply read what you've written. You want to present your ideas forcefully—and that requires animation and eye contact, not having your head stuck in a manuscript. Also, turning a number of pages of notes in front of your audience can be awkward. Those who use manuscripts well have prepared and practiced thoroughly enough that they aren't tied to their manuscript.

If you decide to draw your presentation together by writing out a manuscript, you will need to find a style that works for you. Some presenters prefer to start with their opening and write out their whole presentation straight through, from beginning to end. Others find it works better to write out the main body of the presentation and then go back and add on the opening and closing. Try both approaches to see what works best for you.

Also, beware of writer's block. One place you could get stuck is facing a blank page and not knowing where to begin. If that happens, start anywhere—opening, body, conclusion, or prime illustration. Just grab hold at some place and start writing. Once you've started writing, the rest will usually flow. Remember, you can always rewrite—your first draft doesn't have to be perfect. For that matter, neither does your last draft. The goal isn't perfection—it's excellence.

Get started by completing the Apply It Now! exercise on the next page.

"All planning must eventually degenerate into work for anything to actually happen."

—Peter F. Drucker

Apply It Now!

Write Out Your Presentation

Think about the case study presentation you identified in Chapter 1. Experiment with writing out a portion of it. Pick one of your main points and write out that section, including any illustrations.

_____

_____

_____

_____

_____

_____

_____

_____

_____

Once you've finished, ask yourself:

- Did it help to write it out?

- Did it help me organize my ideas?

- Did it help me to get a better sense of the flow of the material?

- Would writing a manuscript be a good way for me to approach the whole presentation?

Using Both a Manuscript and an Outline

Some presenters prefer to use a combination of outlining and a manuscript. You can write your manuscript, and then outline it and use only the outline notes for your actual presentation. This way you get the benefit of the thoroughness of preparation that a manuscript affords, with the flexibility and immediacy of an outline.

Another approach is to outline your presentation and then write out in full either the whole talk or at least those sections where precision of expression is especially important. Then write a revised outline to actually use at the time of your presentation.

Memorizing Your Presentation

In a word, "Don't!" It's too much work, plus it doesn't work well. Inexperienced presenters are tempted to resort to memorization for the sense of control it gives them. They know exactly what they are going to say and that reduces anxiety. But it creates anxiety of its own when you're trying to get a talk down word perfect. Memorizing your presentation focuses your energy on remembering what comes next, rather than on your ideas, your audience, and how you're communicating with them. Also, if you've memorized your talk and then stumble and lose your place, it can create panic of a high order. It's far better to have a very clear sense of what you're going to say, a good outline or manuscript at hand, and freedom from the chains of memorization. However using notes—whether they're in the form of an outline or a manuscript, isn't at all a liability in most presentations. The exception would be if you're doing a dramatic monologue or some other kind of presentation in which mobility and spontaneity are the most important considerations.

Practice, Practice, Practice

Whether you have settled on the use of an outline or a manuscript, it's essential to practice your presentation. Practicing means standing up and actually saying your presentation out loud, pretending to be in front of your audience. This helps you get a sense of the rhythm and flow of your talk. You get used to the sound of your voice. You get comfortable with your material. After some practice, you can focus on fine-tuning key areas.

You may want to consider practicing in front of a mirror so you can see how you look. Or better yet, videotape yourself. If you have a willing friend, colleague, or spouse, ask them to listen to your presentation and critique it. Suggest they find two affirming things to say for every one criticism. You need to be aware of what you're doing right as well as what needs some polish. At least once, do a dress rehearsal. Put on the clothes you will wear on the day of the presentation and wear them as you go through your talk. This will help you know if you've picked the right outfit. It also eliminates one more new factors to have to adjust to on the big day.

On the actual day of your presentation, try to arrive at the setting early. See if the accommodations are suitable for you and your audience. Find a quiet place if you can, and go over your notes. Take a few moments to get quiet and centered. Visualize yourself as successful. After all, you've prepared well and practiced for this very occasion. You've done your homework. Now it's time to reap the rewards of your successful preparation. Appendix D is a Last-Minute Checklist for you to consult.

When the moment comes, speak out with confidence. Having prepared thoroughly, give your presentation your best effort. Set aside every thought but your audience and how you can connect with them. If you've done your homework, everything will go well. Far better, in fact, than you probably believe at this point.

The time has come to say something. Get up and say it, knowing you really do have something to say!

Key Idea Chart

1. The two main approaches to organizing your presentation are to outline it or to write a manuscript.

2. It's not a good idea to memorize your presentation.

3. It's always a good idea to practice your presentation out loud.

4. Write out below the key idea you got for yourself from Chapter 8.

_____

_____

_____

_____

_____

_____

_____

_____

_____

_____

_____

_____

Audience Awareness Checklist

1. Estimated Size of Audience:

    12 or fewer ____   13-25   ____   26-50   _____

    51-100   ____   101-200   ____   201 or larger   _____

2. Which best describes your audience? (Check as many as apply.)

    _____   People you work with on daily or regular basis

    _____   Clients or customers with whom you have history

    _____   New client or customer

    _____   Civic or community organization

    _____   Open, public forum

    _____   Management group

    _____   People you manage or supervise

    _____   Professional or trade organization

    _____   Other (specify) _____

3. Which best describes the educational background of your audience?

_____ High school degree

_____ College degree

_____ Graduate degree

_____ Technical or professional training

_____ Varied, mixed background

4. What is your estimate of the percentage of females and males?

Female _____%   Male _____%

5. What is likely to be the ethnic or racial composition of your audience?

_____

_____

6. Which of the following describes the nature of your relationship with this audience?

_____ Extensive history, good trust basis

_____ Extensive history, mixed relationships, some conflictive

_____ Some history and reasonably good relationships

_____ Some history, mixed relationships, some conflictive

_____ No history, but you come recommended to them

_____ No history—they don't know you, you don't know them

_____ Public forum

_____ Adversarial relationship

_____ Other (specify) _____

7. Which best describes your comfort level with this particular audience?

_____ Very comfortable, relaxed

_____ Somewhat comfortable

_____ A little anxious

_____ Very anxious, concerned

8. How familiar will your audience likely be with the material you are to present?

_____ Very familiar, shared area of interest, work, or concern

_____ Somewhat familiar

_____ Will probably only have vague acquaintance with this topic

_____ Totally unfamiliar with what you will present

_____ Mixed group, widely varying degrees of familiarity, expertise

9. What particular needs, concerns, interests, issues, or questions will this audience likely be bringing to your presentation? List these below. Be as specific and concrete as possible.

_____

_____

_____

_____

_____

_____

_____

A Twelve-Step Presentation Planner

Step One: Specify Definite Logistics.

Date: _____

Time: _____

Location: _____

Length of presentation: _____

Target date to have preparation completed: _____

Step Two: Attend to the Preliminaries.

1. Know Your Audience—The Who

   Complete the "Audience Awareness Checklist (Appendix A, p. 177).

2. Define Your Purpose—The Why

   Which of the following describes the overall purpose of this presentation?

   _____ Inform, share information

   _____ Decide on a plan of action or appropriate strategy

_____ Analyze and identify key issues or the main problem

_____ Entertain

_____ Inspire or motivate

_____ Sell an idea, product, service

_____ Recommend a plan of action

_____ Do skill training

_____ Do a progress report, update

_____ Do problem solving

_____ Other (specify) _____

3. Fit the Occasion—The Where

Think about your upcoming presentation. Will it be a formal business presentation to a small group? A lecture to a large audience? An informal gathering? Write a brief description of the social setting of your presentation.

_____

_____

_____

_____

_____

_____

_____

_____

Step Three: Narrow Your Focus.

1. Write your theme statement. What is the one, central idea you want to communicate?

_____

_____

_____

2. Write your purpose statement. How are you asking your audience to change?

_____

_____

_____

Step Four: Gather and Organize Your Material.

1. Draw together the necessary resources for your presentation:

   • Review materials you already have on file.

   • Brainstorm creative ideas for your presentation.

   • Research and gather additional information.

   • Set a target date by which you want to have all your material gathered so you'll have time to let it simmer.

2. Write a Possible Points List. Considering all the information you have and the research you've done, what key ideas seem most important and pertinent?

_____

_____

_____

_____

3. Distill your key points. From the Possible Points list you just created, distill down a list of the few key points that are most important to present.

_____

_____

_____

4. Do a preliminary outline of your presentation.

_____

_____

_____

Step Five: Add Life and Interest to Your Presentation.

1. Identify any investments, values, or convictions you bring to this presentation. Complete the following sentences:

• I feel strongly about…

• It is important to me that…

- People need to understand that I…

- The most important thing for me about this presentation is…

2. Identify one or more illustrations for each of your key points. Consider examples, analogies, comparisons and contrasts, object lessons, anecdotes, and stories.

3. Identify any points in your presentation that would lend themselves to humor. Think of an appropriate quip, anecdote, or joke to fit.

4. What visual aids will you be using? List them. Set completion dates for each item.

Aid	*Date*
_____	_____
_____	_____
_____	_____
_____	_____
_____	_____

Step Six: Write Your Opening.

1. Either write out or outline in detail your opening.

2. Evaluate it.

- Will it get your audience's attention?

- Does it establish a common ground with your audience?

- Does it alert the audience to your theme and direction?

Step Seven: Write Your Ending.

1. Either write out or outline in detail your ending.

2. Evaluate it.

   • Does it summarize your main points and theme?

   • Does it make clear to your audience what action you are asking them to take or what change you are asking them to make?

Step Eight: Examine Your Transitions.

1. Are the transitions between your main points clear?

2. Do you need to note for yourself specific transitional phrases to use?

Step Nine: Prepare for Questions and Objections.

1. List out the questions you think your audience is most likely to raise. Think through your response should those questions come up. Should any of them be incorporated into your presentation?

2. List out possible objections that may be raised. Think through your responses. Prepare yourself for anticipated objections.

Step Ten: Draw Your Presentation Together.

1. Either outline your presentation in detail or write it out in manuscript form.

2. Reduce your manuscript or detailed outline into a set of notes for your presentation.

Step Eleven: Practice!

1. Practice your presentation aloud a number of times until you begin to feel comfortable with it.

2. Go back and fine-tune places that seem uneven or otherwise in need of improvement.

3. Consider finding a friend or colleague who will listen to your presentation and critique you.

Step Twelve: Visualize Your Success.

You are going to do great! You've prepared well. You are on the road to making a powerful and successful presentation. Picture your success and rehearse your presentation mentally a number of times.

Facilities Checklist

Signs and Directions

_____ Do the participants know where the meeting will be held?

_____ Are there signs and directions in lobby areas?

_____ Is the entrance clearly marked?

Seating

_____ Is there an adequate number of chairs available?

_____ Are they arranged in a way conducive to the presentation?

_____ Will everyone be able to see you, the screen (if you're using one), and other visual aids?

Sound System

_____ Will you be using amplified sound?

_____ Have you tested and adjusted the system?

_____ Do you know how to adjust it or the appropriate person to contact should further adjustments be required?

_____ If you are using a wireless microphone, are additional batteries on hand?

Audiovisual Equipment

_____ Have you tested your overhead projector, computer equipment, slide projector, and other equipment?

_____ Are additional bulbs on hand?

_____ Have you tested the screen placement from all points of the room?

_____ If you're using a white board or flip chart, are your pens new?

Temperature

_____ Is the room temperature comfortable? Will it still be so when the room is full of people?

_____ Do you know how to make any necessary adjustments or the appropriate person to call to have adjustments made to room temperature?

Handouts

_____ If you will be using handouts, do you have an adequate number?

_____ Do you want to pass them out during the meeting, have them available as people enter, or already distributed to individual seats?

Facilities Manager

_____ If you're meeting in a hotel or public facility, do you know the name of the banquet manager or facilities manager and how to contact that person should a need arise?

Last-Minute Checklist

_____ Do I have my notes in order?

_____ Is the sound system working properly?

_____ Do I have my overhead transparencies, slides, or other audiovisuals in order?

_____ Have I checked my appearance in a mirror? Checked all zippers?

_____ Have I put a smile on my face?

_____ Have I taken a few moments to get quiet and centered?

_____ Have I visualized myself presenting powerfully and successfully?

Training and Speaker Organizations

American Society for Training and Development, 1443, 1640 King Street, Alexandria, VA 22313, (703) 683-8100.

National Speakers Association, 1500 South Priest Drive, Tempe, AZ 85281, (602) 968-2552, Fax (602) 968-0911.

National Storytelling Association, P.O. Box 309, Jonesborough, TN 37659, (615) 753-2171, Fax (615) 753-9331.

Toastmasters International, P.O. Box 9052, Mission Viejo, CA 92690, (714) 858-8255.

Bibliography and Suggested Resources

Arredondo, Lani. *How to Present Like a Pro*. New York: McGraw Hill, 1991.

McGraw, Robert. *Learning to Laugh at Work: The Power of Humor in the Workplace*. Mission, KS: SkillPath Publications, 1995.

Rabb, Margaret Y., Editor. *The Presentation Design Book: Projecting a Good Image With Your Desktop Computer*. Chapel Hill, NC: Ventana Press, 1990.

Raines, Claire. *Visual Aids in Business*. Los Altos, California: Crisp Publications, 1989.

Varga, Mari Pat. *Great Openings and Closings*. Mission, KS: SkillPath Publications, 1996.

Wilder, Claudyne. *The Presentations Kit: 10 Steps for Selling Your Ideas*. New York: John Wiley & Sons, 1990.

Available From
SkillPath Publications

Self-Study Sourcebooks

Climbing the Corporate Ladder: What You Need to Know and Do to Be a Promotable Person *by Barbara Pachter and Marjorie Brody*

Coping With Supervisory Nightmares: 12 Common Nightmares of Leadership and What You Can Do About Them *by Michael and Deborah Singer Dobson*

Defeating Procrastination: 52 Fail-Safe Tips for Keeping Time on Your Side *by Marlene Caroselli, Ed.D.*

Discovering Your Purpose *by Ivy Haley*

Going for the Gold: Winning the Gold Medal for Financial Independence *by Lesley D. Bissett, CFP*

Having Something to Say When You Have to Say Something: The Art of Organizing Your Presentation *by Randy Horn*

Info-Flood: How to Swim in a Sea of Information Without Going Under *by Marlene Caroselli, Ed.D.*

The Innovative Secretary *by Marlene Caroselli, Ed.D.*

Mastering the Art of Communication: Your Keys to Developing a More Effective Personal Style *by Michelle Fairfield Poley*

Organized for Success! 95 Tips for Taking Control of Your Time, Your Space, and Your Life *by Nanci McGraw*

A Passion to Lead! How to Develop Your Natural Leadership Ability *by Michael Plumstead*

P.E.R.S.U.A.D.E.: Communication Strategies That Move People to Action *by Marlene Caroselli, Ed.D.*

Productivity Power: 250 Great Ideas for Being More Productive *by Jim Temme*

Promoting Yourself: 50 Ways to Increase Your Prestige, Power, and Paycheck *by Marlene Caroselli, Ed.D.*

Proof Positive: How to Find Errors Before They Embarrass You *by Karen L. Anderson*

Risk-Taking: 50 Ways to Turn Risks Into Rewards *by Marlene Caroselli, Ed.D. and David Harris*

Stress Control: How You Can Find Relief From Life's Daily Stress *by Steve Bell*

The Technical Writer's Guide *by Robert McGraw*

Total Quality Customer Service: How to Make It Your Way of Life *by Jim Temme*

Write It Right! A Guide for Clear and Correct Writing *by Richard Andersen and Helene Hinis*

Your Total Communication Image *by Janet Signe Olson, Ph.D.*

Handbooks

The ABC's of Empowered Teams: Building Blocks for Success *by Mark Towers*

Assert Yourself! Developing Power-Packed Communication Skills to Make Your Points Clearly, Confidently, and Persuasively *by Lisa Contini*

Breaking the Ice: How to Improve Your On-the-Spot Communication Skills *by Deborah Shouse*

The Care and Keeping of Customers: A Treasury of Facts, Tips, and Proven Techniques for Keeping Your Customers Coming BACK! *by Roy Lantz*

Challenging Change: Five Steps for Dealing With Change *by Holly DeForest and Mary Steinberg*

Dynamic Delegation: A Manager's Guide for Active Empowerment *by Mark Towers*

Every Woman's Guide to Career Success *by Denise M. Dudley*

Great Openings and Closings: 28 Ways to Launch and Land Your Presentations With Punch, Power, and Pizazz *by Mari Pat Varga*

Hiring and Firing: What Every Manager Needs to Know *by Marlene Caroselli, Ed.D. with Laura Wyeth, Ms.Ed.*

How to Be a More Effective Group Communicator: Finding Your Role and Boosting Your Confidence in Group Situations *by Deborah Shouse*

How to Deal With Difficult People *by Paul Friedman*

Learning to Laugh at Work: The Power of Humor in the Workplace *by Robert McGraw*

Making Your Mark: How to Develop a Personal Marketing Plan for Becoming More Visible and More Appreciated at Work *by Deborah Shouse*

Meetings That Work *by Marlene Caroselli, Ed.D.*

The Mentoring Advantage: How to Help Your Career Soar to New Heights *by Pam Grout*

Minding Your Business Manners: Etiquette Tips for Presenting Yourself Professionally in Every Business Situation *by Marjorie Brody and Barbara Pachter*

Misspeller's Guide *by Joel and Ruth Schroeder*

Motivation in the Workplace: How to Motivate Workers to Peak Performance and Productivity *by Barbara Fielder*

NameTags Plus: Games You Can Play When People Don't Know What to Say *by Deborah Shouse*

Networking: How to Creatively Tap Your People Resources *by Colleen Clarke*

New & Improved! 25 Ways to Be More Creative and More Effective *by Pam Grout*

Power Write! A Practical Guide to Words That Work *by Helene Hinis*

The Power of Positivity: Eighty ways to energize your life *by Joel and Ruth Schroeder*

Putting Anger to Work For You *by Ruth and Joel Schroeder*

Reinventing Your Self: 28 Strategies for Coping With Change *by Mark Towers*

Saying "No" to Negativity: How to Manage Negativity in Yourself, Your Boss, and Your Co-Workers *by Zoie Kaye*

The Supervisor's Guide: The Everyday Guide to Coordinating People and Tasks *by Jerry Brown and Denise Dudley, Ph.D.*

Taking Charge: A Personal Guide to Managing Projects and Priorities *by Michal E. Feder*

Treasure Hunt: 10 Stepping Stones to a New and More Confident You! *by Pam Grout*

A Winning Attitude: How to Develop Your Most Important Asset! *by Michelle Fairfield Poley*

For more information, call 1-800-873-7545.

Notes

Notes

Notes

Notes

Notes

Notes